RELATIONSHIP ADVICE FOR COUPLES WORKBOOK

RULES
&
ROSES

Take Your Relationship To The Next Level

Alex Miller

Table of Contents

PART 1 4
Chapter 1: 6 Relationship Goals To Have 5
Chapter 2: 7 Ways To Keep Your Relationship Fresh and Exciting 9
Chapter 3: 7 Ways To Live Together In Harmony With Your Partner 14
Chapter 4: Stop Setting Unrealistic Expectations of Your Partner 19
Chapter 5: 7 Signs That You're Ready To Take Your Relationship To The Next Level 22
Chapter 6: What To Do When You Are At Different Life Stages In A Relationship 27
Chapter 7: 7 Ways To Keep Your Relationship Fresh 31
Chapter 8: 6 Tips To Find The One 36
Chapter 9: 10 Ways To Build A Strong Relationship 40
PART 2 48
Chapter 1: 7 Signs Of An Incompatible Relationship 49
Chapter 2: 6 Ways To Deal With Arguments In A Relationship 55
Chapter 3: 9 Tips To Have A Healthy Long Distance Relationship 59
Chapter 4: 6 Signs Your Love Is One-Sided 63
Chapter 5: 7 Ways To Become A Good Partner 67
Chapter 6: 6 Crazy Ways People Have Met Their Soulmates 72
Chapter 7: Make Time for Your Partner 77
Chapter 8: 7 Ways To Be More Mature In A Relationship 80
Chapter 9: 7 Ways To Deal With An Overly Jealous Partner 84
Chapter 10: 8 Signs That Someone Is Not Your Soulmate 89
PART 3 93
Chapter 1: 6 Ways To Deal With Betrayal 94
Chapter 2: 7 Ways To Deal With Growing Apart In A Relationship ... 98
Chapter 3: What To Do When You Have Thoughts of Breaking Up 103

Chapter 4: 7 Ways To Deal With Sexual Problems In A Relationship 106

Chapter 5: 6 Signs You Have A Fear of Intimacy 110

Chapter 6: 7 Ways To Achieve Harmony In Personal Relationships. 114

Chapter 7: 6 Ways To Be More Confident In Bed 119

Chapter 8: 6 Steps To Recover From A Breakup 123

Chapter 9: 6 Signs You Are Ready To Move To The Next Step In A Relationship 127

Chapter 10: 7 Signs You Have Found A Keeper 131

PART 1

Chapter 1:
6 Relationship Goals To Have

We live in a generation where the term "relationship goals" has become a part of the trendy vernacular. It may seem more like a hashtag than anything else, but we all are eager to go into the depth of its meaning. A beautiful photo of a stunning couple having a good time together? Relationship goals. A cute text message sent to a girlfriend from his boyfriend? Relationship goals. A perfect wedding? Relationship goals. All these might seem sweet and enviable and look like an absolute dream, and it doesn't mean that these come off as accessible to them. If you have ever been in a relationship, you would know exactly what I'm saying.

Love is not always fireworks, passion, and butterflies. Relationships are not just date nights, kisses, and cuddles. And love is not that glamorous as it looks on social media. But when you strive to build something together, involving your selflessness, commitment, and even sweat and tears, those are actual relationship goals. Here is a list of what relationship goals you must have with your partner.

1. Always Do New Things Together

Sure, alone time might be great, but together time is where the magic happens too. Avoiding your relationship becoming mundane and a rut, you both should try to do new things together. This could be choosing any vacation spot or having an exciting adventure together. You both should make a list of all the things you want to do with each other and keep adding stuff that might pop later. Tick things off as you go, and you'll never run out of things to do together.

2. Be Each Other's Biggest Supporters

Perhaps one of the best things about being in a relationship is that you'll always have someone in your corner. Regardless of how crazy or unrealistic your dreams and goals may sound, your partner should be your biggest supporter. Seeing the person you love believing in could come off as a massive motivation to achieve your goals. This goes both ways; both men and women need to feel emotionally supported. You both should take some time out to discuss what emotional support looks like to you, what and when you need it, and then provide the said support for each other.

3. Put Each Other First

Putting each other first in your relationship will ensure that you're paying attention to each other's needs and making sure they are being met. You have become selfless with each other, and you both strive to make each other happy and would do anything to put a smile on each other's faces. You complement each other, protect each other, support and love each other, no matter the obstacles or circumstances.

4. Know The Importance of Alone Time

As much as you don't want to keep your hands off your partner in the early stages of your relationship, it's essential to know that you both need time alone to recharge and refill your cup. Spending all of your time together isn't sustainable, and alone time is significant. It will help you maintain your individuality, allow you breathing space, and encourage a closer relationship with each other when you spend time together.

5. Keep The Physical Connection Going

Sex isn't always an option when dealing with different phases of your relationship. There are going to be times when it might not be physically or mentally possible. But this in no way means that you should stop all physical connections. Physically touching the person you love releases an oxytocin hormone; this feel-good love hormone reduces stress and makes you feel wonderful things. You can stay physically connected by holding hands, cuddling, or simply leaning on one another.

6. Speak Positively About Each Other

Speaking ill of your partner with others is not only disrespectful to them, but it's also disrespectful to your relationship. Sure, you can vent in tough times, but make sure you talk about the actions and behaviors that upset you and not their personality traits. Always speak positively and kindly of each other. Even if their behavior irritates you, focus more on the characteristics you love of them and let it pass.

Conclusion

Relationships are complicated but beautiful at the same time. As simple as the above factors may sound to you, these things take a lot of effort and hard work to be implemented. But when you do all of these with the person you love the most in the world, then all of it can be worth it.

Chapter 2:
7 Ways To Keep Your Relationship Fresh and Exciting

At the beginning of a relationship, one can feel the excitement and the sparks that come from the newness of a relationship. For example, the butterflies you feel before going on a date can make you feel surprisingly on top of the world. It is the start of a relationship that makes you feel this way. At the beginning of a relationship, everything feels fresh as your partner surprises you and makes you feel special.

But as time goes on, the relationship becomes boring. This can often lead to an end of a relationship; to prevent this, you could always keep your relationship fresh and exciting. Even though now both of you are not the same person you used to be in each other's eyes, but you could still maintain that tingly sensation by trying to be more surprising.

Here are seven ways to keep your relationship fresh and exciting.

1. Keep Surprising Each Other

At the start of every relationship, partners often surprise each other with flowers, gifts, or a surprise date. These surprises cause the other partner to feel beloved. Still, people usually stop surprising their partners with such things as time goes on. By continuing to surprise your partner with gifts, flowers, and sweet notes, you keep your relationship fresh. After a while, you learn about the likes and dislikes of your partner. You can easily use that to your advantage by buying them flowers they like or small presents that make them happy. The happiness caused by these small gestures of love can keep the relationship from becoming dull. So don't let the element of surprise die.

2. Ask Them Out On A Date

A relationship often begins with a date, and the date makes you feel nervous and excited. Meeting your partner for the first few times can make you want to look the best version of yourself and continue your efforts to look and be the best for your partners. So don't stop the efforts. Ask your partner out on a fancy date to make them happy. Even if you are just ordering food from outside, you could still light up some candles and set the table with a fancy dinner set.

This could make your partner feel special, and the freshness of the relationship doesn't die with time.

3. Try Something New Together

Always try to do something new, like watching movies you liked as a teenager or eating something you haven't tried before; it awakes the excitement your partner feels throughout the day. Try going ice skating or skateboarding together as a fun activity, taking time from your adult routine, and going hiking and other activities to have fun together simply.

4. Speak About Your Feelings Towards Them

Try voicing your thoughts about them. Don't shy away from words and tell them or remind them regularly how much they mean to you or how strongly you feel towards them; simple sentences like "I love you" can profoundly affect your partner. Please don't take your partner for granted but make them feel good about themselves and tell them how important they are in your life. This can make them appreciate your presence, and the relationship will remain fresh.

5. Set Life Goals Together

You and your partner can decide on some goals that you can achieve together as a couple. It can be any goal, as a financial goal, or exploring the world together. You could save money for vacations together. During this journey, you can motivate each other but can still have fun. Moreover, when you work as a team, it will also strengthen your bond.

6. Turn Off Your Phone

When spending time with each other, try turning off your phone. This will show your partner how important they are to you. Focus on their words and respond actively. Studies show that a relationship can end when you are more focused on social media apps than on your partner. Using too many social media apps can distance you from your partner; try spending more time with them than using your mobile phone and reestablish your bond with them.

7. Greet Each Other With Excitement

When a relationship begins, we often see couples embracing each other with love and passion even when they met just yesterday.

Still, as time passes, couples can be seen greeting each other with just a simple hello or a short hug. Greeting your partner with excitement and enthusiasm can make them long to meet you. They would be excited all day long because of the way you greet them. This can ensure that the excitement of the relationship doesn't die. You can greet them with a warm, comforting hug or simply a few exciting words; saying mushy things can also make them feel loved, like "I missed you" when they come back home from work.

By following the above ways, you can keep your partner happy and your relationship fresh and exciting.

Chapter 3:
7 Ways To Live Together In Harmony With Your Partner

A harmonious relationship can make a person's life happy and beautiful, but, unfortunately, not all of us are blessed with a harmonious relationship. It is essential to work on your relationship in order to make it work. Creating a harmonious bond between you and your partner can make your relationship more healthy and stable. The dream relationship of everybody is to feel loved, accepted, and respected but to achieve such a relationship, and you need to first work on yourself. You need to make sure that you are doing your best at making your partner feel loved.

Most people nowadays want to find their soulmates, but even when they see their soulmates, they don't have a peaceful relationship; the lack of harmony causes this.

Here are 7 ways to live together in harmony with your partner.

1. Accept Your Partners The Way They Are

The first step to a harmonious relationship is acceptance. It would be best to accept your partners the way they are; distancing them from yourself because of a simple mistake can lead to a toxic relationship. If you choose to love a person and be with them, you need to accept the good and bad in them. As they say that no one is perfect, we all are a work in progress. When you cannot receive your partner the way they are, a harmonious relationship cannot be achieved. It would help if you allowed them to evolve and support them throughout this journey.

2. Be Gentle And Compassionate

When you embody gentleness and compassion, your relationship bond deepens, and there is harmony in the relationship. Instead of jumping to conclusions and reacting dramatically, you need to respond with gentleness and understand your partner's feelings. Compassion brings grace to a person. To achieve a harmonious relationship, you should give your partner grace to work on themselves, understand, and give them space to evolve and mature. It may take time, but it strengthens a relationship.

3. Expectations Should Be Released

With expectations comes disappointment. Expectations are the unspoken standards you expected your partner to live up to. When your partner does not live up to your expectations, you might feel upset or disappointed, but how can you have such high expectations from your partner about things that are unspoken. Work on letting go of these ideals that the society and your subconscious mind created about how a relationship should be. Release the attachment to situations turning out a specific way. Brace yourself for different outcomes of different situations. Don't expect too much from your partner because your partner, like you, cannot always live up to your expectation.

4. Personal Space In A Relationship

Every human being needs personal space; we often see couples that are always together. It may feel exciting and comforting at first, but everyone needs their personal space to think and function properly. After being with each other with no personal space, one can start feeling suffocated and may behave negatively. It would help if you had time to breathe, to expand, and to look within. To evolve, you need space. Personal space between couples proves that their relationship is healthy and robust.

5. Honesty

Honest communication is not just a factor to achieve a harmonious relationship but also to have any relationship at all. Not being truthful can cause conflicts and problems in a relationship. Moreover, being a liar can be a toxic trait that can cause your partner to end the relationship. But before being honest with your partner, you need to be honest with yourself. Know your true self, explore the good and bad in yourself. Don't hide your mistakes from your partner; instead, be honest and apologize to them before it is too late. Honesty is a crucial factor in achieving a harmonious relationship.

6. Shun Your Ego

Ego and harmony cannot simply go hand in hand; where ego exists, harmony cannot be established. Often by some people, ego is considered a toxic trait. This is the ego that stops a person from apologizing for his mistakes, which can create tension among the couple. The stubbornness to do things your way is caused by ego and can easily result in unwanted scenarios. These are not the components of a healthy relationship. So to establish a harmonious relationship, you should remove ego and learn to compromise a bit. By removing ego, you allow yourself to be more flexible and understanding.

7. Let Go if Unnecessary Emotional Pain

When you keep hurting over old resentments, you convert that pain into toxic feelings that are not good for a relationship. These poisonous feelings can make you make some bad decisions that may result in your partner feeling unsafe around you. This pain can cause you to bury your positives feeling inside. As a result of this, you may feel pessimistic and may exaggerate minor conflicts into something more. A person must let go of this emotional stress and pain. You can let go by going to a therapist or yoga and meditation. Once you have let go of the pain, your heart is now open to a peaceful and harmonious relationship.

To establish a harmonious relationship, you have to accept and understand your partner and work on yourself. Also, work on your radical integrity.

Chapter 4:
Stop Setting Unrealistic Expectations of Your Partner

Are you wondering how to stop unmet expectations from ruining your relationship? Do you find yourself constantly disappointed with your partner and thinking about ending it?

There are ways to stop unmet expectations from ruining your relationship. Here are a few.

1. Identify Your Own

One way to stop unmet expectations from ruining your relationship is by questioning your own. What do you think you need from your partner? Do you need him to give up his friends and hobbies for you? Do you expect to have sex every night? Do you want her to keep the house spotlessly clean as your mother did? Do you expect him to anticipate your every need?

Expectations like these are exactly the things that can kill a relationship. I would encourage you to think about what you want from your partner so that it's clear in your mind. I also want you to consider if your expectations are reasonable.

If your expectations aren't reasonable, your relationship might be dead upon arrival. If you don't know your expectations, your partner will have a hard time reaching them because you might always be moving the goal post. So, before unmet expectations destroy your relationship, make sure you know what yours are.

2. Set Boundaries

I always encourage new couples to set boundaries in their relationships as soon as possible To understand healthy relationship boundaries, look at the four walls of your house. Those walls are the structure that holds your life together. They hold your food and your bed and your possessions, and it's where you live your life.

Healthy boundaries are the same as those four walls of your house. They are the things that support your relationship as it matures. To have a healthy relationship that can grow and be fruitful, it must have structures and boundaries that support it. Healthy boundaries come in many shapes, sizes, and colors.

A few examples:

- Make sure you stay yourself
- Allow yourselves time apart
- Communication is important
- Mutual respect at all times

- Keep the power dynamic equal
- Making time for both sides of the family
- Respecting others friends and hobbies

Of course, each couple needs to decide what works for them, but every couple must establish some boundaries early and stick to them for the sake of their relationship.

3. Be Truthful

You must discuss this with your partner if your expectations aren't being met. One of the most common complaints that I hear from women is 'he should know what I need. I shouldn't have to tell him.' And this, I am afraid, is mostly impossible. Men would love to anticipate and meet our needs, but many of them just don't always have it in them. This is not some deficiency of character but because men have no idea how women think and why. It's a mystery to them, so expecting them to be able to do so will set you up for disaster.

Chapter 5:
7 Signs That You're Ready To Take Your Relationship To The Next Level

If you're dating someone long enough, chances are you might know them well now and are ready to take your relationship to the next level. You both work out well together through all the ups and downs, connect with each other, and make each other's life wonderful. So whether you're thinking about making your relationship official by introducing them to your family and friends, moving in with them, or even getting engaged, it can both be scary and exciting when you think about making the relationship serious and taking that leap of faith.

While you should definitely consider if your partner is the perfect match for you, you should also do something that makes sure your partner doesn't slip off your hands. It's essential to keep your feelings honest to yourself and your partner because taking that next step would require being more open, vulnerable, and honest. If you feel that you have a healthy relationship, you can't imagine your life without your partner and are in a good place emotionally, then say no more. Here are some signs to convince you that you should up your game!

1. **You both trust each other fully:**

Being able to trust someone entirely isn't as easy as it sounds, especially in times like these and the world we're living in right now. It's more facile to break someone's trust and betray them rather than being an angel and keeping their secrets. The most significant quality one can look for in a partner is how much they value our trust. If you are confident that your partner will always have your back and you can be weak and vulnerable in front of them, maybe you should consider taking the next step. If you have told something to them in confidence and they don't share the information with anyone, and likewise if you do the same, then you both are fortunate. You should never break your partner's trust and expect the same from them.

2. **You support each other through the good and bad:**

Having someone by your side who you know would always support you, no matter what is nothing short of a blessing. Your partner has always comforted and consoled you through the negative phases and cherished and cheered you through the positive ones. Even if they were dealing with their problems, they made sure you were okay first. People like these are very hard to find. Most of the time, we tend to emotionally drain out or become frustrated by being there for people. But with your partner, you are always ready to lend a helping hand and even an ear, listen to all of their problems and shortcomings and support them every step of the way.

3. You both apologize to each other when needed:

One of the major signs of a toxic relationship is when your partner doesn't apologize or take accountability, even if they know they are wrong. These relationships tend to have a dead end. You might have noticed that your partner admits when wrong and apologizes, even if not straight away; they do it sooner or later. They try to sort out the arguments and fights calmly and try to listen to your point of views and opinions too, instead of forcing theirs on you. They make sure that you're okay after the fight and may even make small gestures to make you feel that they are guilty and you are more important than any of the arguments you both get into. Similarly, you do the same for them. This is an excellent sign that you should definitely step up your relationship to the next level.

4. You give each other space:

You both have a level of freedom and independence both within and outside the relationship. You both aren't on each other's throat and nerves every second. You both have different hobbies and passions that you pursue. You both can meet your friends alone or hang out by yourself, without stressing over if your partner would mind. This is a sign of a healthy relationship when you don't keep buzzing your partner with unlimited calls or texts, ask them about their whereabouts, or cling to them all day. Everyone deserves some free time of their own in which they can be alone and ponder over things.

5. You're on the same page with them:

Even if you and your partner don't share the same goals, hobbies, dreams, passions, or even the same views and opinions, you're still on the same page with them about your values and future. For example, both of you have discussed either having children or no children in the future, getting a destination wedding or a simple one, moving out of the city or across the country, or settling in the same spot where you both are right now. Agreeing on the same stuff shows that you both prioritize the same things and are compatible with stepping up your relationship.

6. You feel safe with them:

One of the signs that your relationship is ready for the next step is the feeling of comfort and security when you are with them. You can be your utter authentic self with them without fearing that they might judge you or dislike you. You have shown all of your sides to them, the good and the bad, and they still love you regardless. They like your quirks and don't get annoyed or irritated by your behavior. You also have accepted your partner's flaws and imperfections and still look at them the same way.

7. Your family and friends love them:

You have introduced them to your family as well as your friends. You were nervous at first as to if they will like them or not. But your partner turned out to be the charmer and swept your family members as well as your close friends off of their feet. They can't help but ask about your partner the minute you visit them and even tease you about taking the next big step with them. They have started to invite your partner on all the occasions and events to spend more time with them and get to know them better. All in all, your family and friends love your partner, and your partner's friends and family do the same to you.

Conclusion:

Taking the next big step in a relationship could be confusing and stressful, especially when you find yourself confused and unclear. But if you want to keep someone in your life forever, you have to make sure you make all the efforts to keep yourself with them. So if you have found someone worthy of your time and energy, don't let them go. Instead, cling onto them, and make efforts to keep your relationship floating.

Chapter 6:
What To Do When You Are At Different Life Stages In A Relationship

If you've started dating someone a lot older or younger than you and you haven't experienced any bumps along the way, it might be because your relationship is still relatively new.

"The issues begin, I think, to manifest themselves when people start to get into real-life situations. For example, if you don't want kids right away and you're dating someone who never wants them, it might not seem like an issue at the beginning. Still, later on, when you start to feel more ready to start a family, understandably, that tiny little thing can become a really big thing.

Not only that, but some people have had issues dating each other because they were at different stages in their lives. For example, while one might want to go out and dance with friends, the other might have no interest in spending time that way.

There are still ways to make a relationship work if you're at different stages in your life.

That doesn't necessarily mean that the relationship can't work just because you have different interests. For example, a woman said that her husband is ten years younger than her, and they don't have the same taste in music. But they each have friends to talk about those kinds of things, and it works for them.

"If you're dating someone with a big age difference, remember the reasons why you are drawn to that person," "Maybe you are very mature, and individuals your age aren't able to connect with you on a deeper level. Maybe you have a fun, energetic side, and you haven't been able to find a partner your age with similar interests and activities."

We advise that you do some reflection about what you want in the relationship to be clear on that and remind yourself of it when necessary.

Make sure your values, morals, and life goals match up.

"If you want the relationship to be long-term, then make sure that your values, morals, and life goals match.

Ask yourself a few specific questions before diving into something. Things like future goals, where you want to live, if you want a family, if you want religion to be part of your life, and if you see this person fitting in with your family and friends.

It's also important to consider what your relationship will look like down the line. "Big age differences aren't as noticeable when you're both middle-aged, but what happens once one of you is a senior, and the other isn't?" "These are the big picture questions that need to be thought about before you decide to spend your life together."

If you agree with each other on the big things, smaller things like having different tastes in music likely won't be as big of a deal. Just like in any relationship, you don't have to (and won't) agree on everything all the time. Although it might seem like you're farther apart on some topics than you would be if you're closer in age, other factors besides age might play a role in that.

Be prepared for others to comment on your relation.

There's a good chance that people will have opinions about your relationship." They'll ask questions, and they'll make comments that are probably pretty annoying, so be prepared with a response. Depending on who the person is, you might actually feel like you can get into an explanation of the relationship, but other times, it might not feel necessary, so just to be prepared with that,"

Ensure that the relationship's dynamic is equal and that one partner doesn't hold power over the other.

Each partner needs to avoid mothering the other, regardless of who's older or younger in the relationship. It can be difficult for those who take on that role, even among friends, to not act that way with their significant other, but she said that it's important to try to refrain. Sometimes mothering can turn into holding power over your partner, which isn't healthy behavior.

Chapter 7:
7 Ways To Keep Your Relationship Fresh

Anyone who's in a relationship wants to know the secret to make their love life last. And while everyone's relationship is different, the couples should thrive to keep the spark alive for years or even decades. Being in love is beautiful on the one hand but complex on the other. It takes a lot of time, sacrifices, effort, and adjustments to nurture a relationship that will leave you happy and satisfied. However, over some time, partners tend to get bored with each other and end up finding ways to keep the relationship excited.

No matter what type of a relationship you are in, be it a marriage, casual dating, or exploring open relationships, the bonds form with another gets more substantial and more meaningful when you explore new things together, have love and respect for each other, and be grateful for each other every day. From the mundane to the extra special, there are many things to keep a relationship fresh and exciting.

Here are 7 ways to keep your relationship fresh.

1. Be Adventurous

It's essential to take risks with your partner to keep things interesting. The key is to be adventurous together and push one another to try new things. Sure, it might sound scary at first, but you will always have your partner to support and push you. If it's something that you have a phobia of, but your partner loves it, try it for their sakes.

2. Show Gratitude

Gratitude goes a long way in any relationship. Simply saying thank you to your partner more often and with a kind the intention will make both you and your partner feel good and closer to each other. Several studies suggest that showing gratitude goes along with lower levels of depression, anxiety, and envy. Appreciate them for their ideas, views, opinions, and the things they do for you, no matter how small or big they may be. Do something special for them to tell them how much they mean to you.

3. Treat As You Want To Be Treated

Give your partner the same things that you wish to receive from them. Whether it's your love, passion, generosity, and kindness, or your quirks, phobias, traumas, and insecurities, loving someone comes with all sorts of nuances. Make sure to ask your partner what they need, and don't hesitate to communicate with your partner clearly and tell them what you want. It would be best if you first were the way you want your partner to be. Treat each other with kindness, respect, and compassion.

4. **Take A Considerable Risk Together**

It may sound a little crazy, but this is exactly what couples need. Switching up your life in a big way can help strengthen your bond with your partner in unimaginable ways. One of the best ways to create a closer connection is to do something risky, like move to a new city, or a state, or even a country. It may sound dramatic, but it all comes down to choosing to face risks together. Whenever life throws at us a difficult choice, we pick the scariest thing and grow through it.

5. **Have Date Nights**

Between your busy life and all the extracurricular stuff, you might think that a date night would sound unnecessary or extravagant. But scheduling a date night would just be what you and your partner need! Date nights are the dedicated times for you and your partner to connect and have fun together. It's an escape from whatever good or bad is going on in your life right now. You can worry about the bills and the to-do lists later. For now, make it all seem to go away and enjoy the time that you two have in hand.

6. Spend Time Alone

Yes, you heard that right. Spend some time alone, without your partner. While we are all about fun date nights and moving to another city, spending time with yourself is equally important. When we have some alone time, we self-analyze and self-reflect and bring all this knowledge of self-awareness to our partner. It helps you connect with yourself on a deeper level and gives you the benefit of looking at yourself and ask, "Am I someone I'd want to be with?"

7. Do The Things They Like (Even If You Don't Like Them Much)

You should accompany your partner from time to time to the things they enjoy doing, even if it's not really your thing. Be it shopping, golfing, swimming, or any other activity, you should take part in it unless there's a specific reason or you not to. Be generous, open-minded, and graceful in what your partner is interested in. Even if it bores you to death, your partner will feel appreciated and happy, and this will bring both of you closer to each other.

Conclusion

Choose to love your partner no matter what. Know that we all are full of flaws, but our true strength lies in accepting the quirks and shortcomings of the people we love. Help them get into a good mood; surprising and appreciating them are vital elements to a lasting relationship. You don't have to go overboard, and just a few small meaningful gestures will suffice.

Chapter 8:
6 Tips To Find The One

Finding someone who matches our criteria can be a difficult task. We always look for a person who is a knight in shining armor. And by time, we make our type. We are finding someone who looks and behaves like our ideal one. We always fantasize about our right one. No matter how hard it may seem to find someone, we should never lose hope. Sharing is always beneficial. And if you trust someone enough to share your life with them, then it's worth the risk to be taken. The person you chose depends upon you only. The advice can only give you an idea, and you have to act on your own.

Now, when looking for someone from scratch can be difficult for many of us. That person can either be the wrong one or the right one. Only time can tell you that. But you both need to grow together to know if you can survive together. And if not, then separation is the only possible way. But if you find the right one, then it will all be good. You have to have faith in yourself. Be your wingman and go after whatever you desire.

1. **Be Patient**

When looking for someone you want to spend your time with, someone you want to dedicate a part of your life to, you have to devote your time looking for the one. Be patient with everyone you meet so you will get to know them better. They will be more open towards you when you give them time to open. Doing everything fast will leave you confused. Don't only talk with them. Notice their habits, share secrets and trust them. They will be more comfortable around you when they think that you are willing to cooperate.

2. **Keep Your Expectations Neutral**

When you find someone for you, they can either leave you disappointed or satisfied. That all depends on your expectations. If you wait for prince charming and get a knight, then you will be nothing but uncomfortable with them. Keep them neutral. Try to make sure that you get to know a person before passing your judgment.

3. Introduce Them To Your Friends

The people who love you tend to get along together. The first thing we do after finding a competitor is telling a friend. We usually go for the people our loved one has chosen for us. While finding the one is all you. They can play a part in giving advice, but they can't decide for you. When we see one, we want everyone to get to know them.

4. Don't Be Discouraged

You are 30 and still haven't found anyone worth your time. If so, then don't get discouraged. That love comes to us when we least expect it. You have to keep looking for that one person who will brighten your days and keep you happy. Please don't go looking for it. It will come to you itself and will make you happy.

5. Look Around You

Sometimes our journey of finding the one can be cut short when we see the one by our side—someone who has been our friend or someone who was with us all along. You will feel happier and more comfortable with finding the right person within your friend. It will make things much more manageable. And one day, you will realize that he was the one all this time. Sometimes we can find one in mutual friends. They may be strangers, but you know a little about them already. However, finding the one within your friend can save you a lot of trouble.

6. Keep The Sparks Fresh

Whatever happens, don't let your spark die because it will become the source of your compassion. It will make a path for you to walk on with your ideal one. Keep that passion, that love alive. If there is no spark, then you will live a life without any light. So, make your partner and yourself feel that compassion in your growth.

Conclusion

Finding one can be a difficult job, but once we find them, they can make us the happiest in the world. And if that person is honest with you, then there is nothing more you should need in one. You can always change your partner until you find the one because they are always their ones too. You have to focus on finding your own.

Chapter 9:
10 Ways To Build A Strong Relationship

Relationships are not always easy, especially when both people aren't exactly on the same page. But the key to a strong and healthy relationship doesn't necessarily mean you guys are mirror images of each other when it comes to your opinions and personality. Understanding and adaptability is the key to a successful relationship.

When it comes down to the two people involved, no two relationships are the same. As we are unique individuals, so will our relationships be as well. The needs, goals, perceptions, and growth vary from couple to couple. With that in mind, we are going to talk about the 10 signs that point to a strong relationship that all couples should strive for at some point in their time together.

1. Trust.

The foundation of any relationship is very much dependent on trust. More than love, trust is more important for the bond to be strong. Trust includes honesty, integrity, and at the same time feeling safe and comfortable with the person that you are with.

Trust has to be earned over time, by proving to your partner that they can count on you to be faithful in the relationship and also to be honest with things that are going on with your life.

Trust is also earned when you work with your partner in the same domain and you have a clear understanding of their passions.

2. Respect for personal space.

I feel that this needs to be heard loud and clear. Being in a relationship does not imply breathing down the neck of your partner all the time.

Doing so could potentially suffocate the other person and make the relationship bitter over time.

I am sure you don't like your personal space to be violated by someone else all the time, so expect the same adverse reactions if you do that to your partner as well.

It is very important that each individual in the relationship has the utmost respect for the other person's private space. Allowing room to breathe can be a wonderful way to recharge and come back to the relationship with renewed excitement and interest.

3. Spending quality time with your partner.

It is very important for two people in a relationship to spend quality time together. A certain time each week that you have set aside for your partner where the two of you will focus only on each other and nothing else. A time when you ask your partner the deep questions, to engage in insightful thought, or to simply be mindfully present in each other's company. It is an amazing feeling when your significant other engages you by asking about your day, asking how you are feeling, and making sure you are well taken care of.

While many thinks that quantity of time is important as well, I would argue that this could lead to complacency. It is important that you don't treat spending time with your partner by counting the hours, but by counting the moments instead.

4. Encouraging each other to achieve personal goals.

When your partner becomes your life coach who motivates you to become a better person every day and achieve your personal goals , this is where the bond grows beyond the surface level feelings into a much deeper emotional and spiritual connection.

By understanding the kind of service you need to provide to your partner to support their goals and dreams, you are in effect helping them achieve what they truly want in life. This proactiveness will make them fall in love with themselves and with you even more.

5. Physical Intimacy.

Physical intimacy doesn't necessarily imply sex. Sex is not necessary for a relationship to stick on provided both sides are on the same page. Even cuddles, hugs, and kissing your partner is an act of intimacy that is very important in any relationship. It is very crucial to have that understanding in the bedroom and to be able to openly express your needs, your desires, and your fantasies, and your inhibitions regarding physical intimacy with your partner. Lack of physical touch could result in loss of intimacy away from the bedroom. So be mindful that you keep that in check in your relationship.

6. Communication.

There is nothing more important than keeping the communication flowing with your partner. If you aren't comfortable in sharing your deepest emotions, fears, and insecurities with that person, you should probably think about why that is so. Your better half should not just be your partner in a relationship but should ideally by a very close and personal friend as well. There should not be inhibitions about expressing one's feelings and opinions about a matter out of fear that it might end up in a fight with the other person. Fights will inevitably happen in every relationship. How you manage the fights is what makes or breaks your strong bond.

7. Teamwork.

A relationship would become a burden if one person is constantly working hard to keep the other person comfortable and the other one doesn't contribute much. As the saying goes, team work makes the dream work. Be it household chores, cleaning the dishes, settling the bills, taking the dog out for a dump, both have to contribute equally for it to be a balanced relationship. Both will need to take the initiative to help out the other party where possible otherwise resentment and unhappiness might follow.

8. Personal Time.

This point overlaps quite a bit with providing personal space.

To be a more balanced individual, you really need to have that "me-time" for yourself. Time where you spend alone. Time where you engage in your favourite hobbies or sports that you might not share with your partner.

Giving yourself that "me-time" can also include having that favorite cup of coffee while watching your favorite shows, catching up with your friends, cooking your favorite meal, or watching your favorite team match. Once you start balancing time for yourself you start respecting your partner's personal space and time as well, and that gives the relationship a breath of fresh air and keeps you both going.

9. Talking to your partner, not to other people.

It is very easy in times of fights to simply run away from the problems you are facing and into your friends for shelter. While having a strong social support network is great to have, always ensure that you come back to the relationship with a clear mind and talk things through openly and without fear of judgement.

Miscommunications are usually high up on the list when it comes to disagreements. It is always best to sort out the differences there instead of running away and letting the situation escalate to an unresolvable point.

10. The 3 golden phrases.

Yes, you are right. In a relationship, you should be able to say 'I am sorry', 'Thank you', and 'I love you' as much as possible. Being able to express your love, regret, appreciativeness, and sorrow, will enlighten the bond between you and your partner. By verbally saying these words regularly, you are showing your partner that you can be vulnerable around them and that they can be the same with you.

A Strong relationship is not easy to build, but it is worth the effort if we take the time and effort to put into practice some of these points that we have discussed today. Take care and I'll see you in the next one.

Rules and Roses

PART 2

Chapter 1:
7 Signs Of An Incompatible Relationship

You might have heard the word 'compatibility' a million times before starting a new relationship or even after getting into one. But what exactly does the word 'compatibility' means? Compatibility is when you and your partner not only share the same interests but also share the same values, goals, have compatible libidos, support each other in their times of distress and frustration, help them achieve their dreams, make each other feel safe, and plan a future where you can both see each other being together and happy. However, not every couple is blessed with the joys of having a compatible relationship. Melody Kiersz, a professional matchmaker, says, "There are some obvious ones, like not wanting the same things in life, lifestyle choices in terms of travel or location, and relationship style (I.e., monogamous vs. Polyamorous)."

No matter how much in love you are with your partner and how desperately you compromise in your relationship to make everything seem better, if you both aren't compatible, then the relationship might have a dead-end in the long run. Here are some signs that will help you see if you are in an incompatible relationship.

1. Your partner doesn't respect the differences:

There's rarely a time when you might feel that you have found a person just like you. People are different from each other. Sometimes, their passion or goals may align with yours, but some differences are always there. You may like to read a book or watch a movie in your free time instead of your partner playing a video game or going outdoor with their friends. If your partner doesn't respect the differences and forces you to change your hobbies and dreams, then it's a red flag. After all, respect is the critical element to any lasting relationship. In an incompatible relationship, your partner might make you feel bad about being different from them and may mock you about the different things you do.

2. Your partner gets overly jealous:

We, as human beings, cannot wholly eliminate the factor of jealousy from within ourselves. Being jealous and possessive of your partner isn't a bad thing, as long as you have it under control. But if your partner gets overly jealous of petty things, keeps a regular check on you and your whereabouts, and constantly bugs you, then it will not only make you frustrated, but you will eventually be exhausted, and your mental health will shamble. This isn't just a sign of incompatibility but also a sign of toxicity.

3. You're a different version of yourself around them:

What is a relationship if you don't even feel comfortable around your partner? Out of all the people, your love interest should be the one with whom you can be yourself and not pretend. You find yourself always pretending to be a perfect flawless creature because they might have said something or showed you that they wouldn't accept the things that your real version does. The constant struggle of making yourself look ideal in Infront of your partner's eyes would eventually drain you out. You might stop pretending after a while, and your partner may or may not like it. If your partner doesn't like the real you, then you should consider this as an incompatible relationship and move on.

4. Lack of communication:

A lasting relationship is based on communicating effectively with your partner. For example, suppose you feel like your partner discards your feelings and consider them stupid after you tell them that something's been bothering you or tells them that something they've said might have hurt you. In that case, your partner is being emotionally unavailable and doesn't value your feelings. As a result, you might feel uneasy about opening up to them, and they might feel the same about you. This is one of the significant reasons for the incompatibility between the partners. If you aren't ready to share your feelings with them or get ignored if you share them, the relationship will eventually come down the hill.

5. **Your partner does not take care of your wants and needs:**

Consider this, and you have just come home after a long day of work, hoping to get some rest. As soon as you arrive, there is a long pile of dishes waiting for you, and your partner tells you to make something for dinner. Yep, you can imagine the reaction your partner would get. A relationship should be based on mutual efforts and understanding. If your partner is doing the bare minimum and you find yourself putting in all the efforts, then you definitely don't deserve to be with a person like them. Instead, your partner should treat you special every now and then, makes you realize your worth in his life, takes care of you, and make small gestures to show his love.

6. **Fighting gets ugly with them:**

Arguing and fighting are the forte of every relationship. What matters is how you resolve the issue after you've argued or fought. In a compatible relationship, couples always try to sort out the things bothering them, and they eventually apologize to each other. While in an incompatible relationship, you would find your partner constantly bickering and mocking long after the fight has ended. You both won't see eye to eye with each other for days and may go to bed angry at each other. Your partner isn't open to change and doesn't respect your views and opinions. You can't agree to disagree with each other and tries to prove the other wrong no matter what. If you find yourself spending more time fighting with your partner than being happy, you clearly are mismatched.

7. **Different outlooks on the future:**

Two people may be in the same relationship, but they rarely are on the same page. While one might be thinking about getting engaged or married soon, the other might flee to the hills just at the mere name of commitment. One might talk about having kids one day while the other just brushes off the idea that they're not ready for that yet. One must be thinking about traveling the world while the other just wants to stay peacefully in the town. It's best to start talking about your future early in the relationship to see where both of you stand in each other's lives.

Conclusion:

The signs mentioned above are all the major red flags of incompatibility. But, in addition, you must have a sense of mutual respect, understanding, and effort with your partner. For example, suppose you feel that the relationship is one-sided, with you giving your all, making sacrifices, trying to be consistent with them. Yet, at the same time, they couldn't care less about you and don't appreciate or value all that you do for them. In that case, you should consider moving out of the relationship for good.

Chapter 2:
6 Ways To Deal With Arguments In A Relationship

Arguments are common in all kinds of relationships, be it with your parents, siblings, friends, or partner. Some degree of conflict can even be healthy as it shows that both of the partners are expressing themselves, rather than keeping their emotions fester and everything inside. Fighting consistently can also lead to a problematic relationship where you and your partner wouldn't be at peace. And if handled poorly, it can also become the cause of the downfall of your relationship.

It's normal to argue with your loved ones from time to time, but if the arguing is continuing at an unhealthy pace, or your disagreements are ending up in hostile silence, or worse, a screaming match, then it can take a severe toll on your life and affect it. Learning ways to handle disagreements constructively must be crucial in every relationship. Conflict is inevitable; it's how you deal with it that counts. Here are some of the ways to deal with arguments in a relationship.

1. **Find Out Why You're Arguing In The First Place**

Sometimes we look at the superficial layer of the issue, not the deeper layers that might discover the real reason behind the argument. If you and your partner frequently argue or about the same things, it can be good to evaluate what really is causing the conflict. You should see if the argument is really what you think you're arguing about, or are other factors involved too? Are there other things happening in your relationship that are worrying or frustrating you? You may want to consider other influences too, like, are there any significant changes happening in your life that's putting extra pressure on you? Maybe you're spending less time with your partner, and the cause of your arguments is sometimes unknown. Or perhaps you're both struggling with something that you aren't ready to talk about. Looking at the broader context of your situation and seeing past your emotions can be a great way to get to the bottom of what's going on.

2. **Talking It Over**

Talking calmly and constructively when you are actually overwhelmed and feeling emotional can be really difficult. It would be best if you gave yourself and your partner some time to cool off before starting the discussion again. It's essential to open up your feelings to your partner and ask them to do the same. If something's bothering you, you can always talk to your partner calmly and understandably rather than keeping it inside and only giving them hints. No one likes a guessing game in a relationship. Being vocal about your issues and hearing about your partner's, and then talking and sorting it out is critical.

3. Try To Start The Discussion Amicably

Don't start bypassing sarcastic or critical comments, mocking them, or aiming them with gun fires. It can only worsen the situation. Your partner may feel like you're insulting them and not respecting their emotions. Don't take the arguments personally and make it all about yourself. Try to be calm and patient and start by saying something positive like, "I feel like we have been arguing a lot lately; maybe we should discuss what's causing us both trouble and get back to our loving selves." This will not only make your partner feel important but also might end the argument all in all.

4. Try To See Things From Your Partner's Perspective

A conversation is likely to end up being productive if both partners aren't ready to listen to each other. It can be tempting to get your point across, but if you're looking to resolve things, you should take the time to hear about your partner's side too. They might have an entirely different perspective, but you need to understand it if you want to get to the root of what's causing you both to fight. Try to validate each other's feelings by hearing each other and comforting each other.

5. Keep Tabs On Physical Feelings

If the argument is getting too heated, take some time out to calm yourself and then continue once you're both feeling better. Don't pass remarks that you might later regret, or it could make your fight worse. It could end up leaving both of you seriously hurt.

6. Be Prepared to Compromise

Giving ground by both partners is often the only way to resolve a conflict. If both of you stick rigidly to your desired outcome, the fight would never come to an end. Sometimes, an imperfect solution can be better than having no solution at all. To move past things, one or both of the partners must compromise a little.

Conclusion

It can take some time and practice to disagree calmly and constructively and to change the negative behaviors. But if you stick with working together better, it can produce positive changes in your relationship. Forgive yourself and your partner and move on.

Chapter 3:
9 Tips To Have A Healthy Long Distance Relationship

Who says long-distance relationships don't last? Well, a lot of your friends and family members would be against it, they would discourage it, and will advise you not to take it too seriously as for them, it'll only lead to your heartbreak. Honestly, it's not going to be easy. Long-distance would make most of the things unachievable, it could get complicated at times, and you will find yourself vulnerable, sad, and lonely. However, that extra distance also plays a role in getting both of you closer. Studies have found that long-distance relationships don't differ significantly from geographically close relationships, and even in some cases, it might even be better.

First of all, you should be comforted in knowing that long-distance relationships can succeed. With that in mind, we have combined a list of tips that will keep your long-distance relationship healthy and ensure that it lasts.

Technology Is Your Best Friend

In this age of facetime-ing and texting without paying sky-high rates, long-distance relationships are now easier than ever. You can share the day-to-day minutia with your partner by instantaneously sharing photos, exchanging texts and calls, and skyping one another. It'sIt's much different than writing a letter to your loved one and waiting weeks or months for a response. People in long-distance relationships also rely more heavily on technology to stay connected with each other. This helps them communicate verbally even more than the couples who see each other often, sit in the same room, and do not interact at all. It's essential not just to generalize but to share details with your partner. It would make both of you feel like you've witnessed each other's day.

Be Commited to The Relationship
This implies to everyone involved in relationships, but especially to people who are pursuing long-distance relationships. It's crucial to know that you're committed to only one person and that you love them before wasting your time as well as theirs. If you're choosing to stay in a long-distance relationship, you both must sort out where you both stand in life, what will happen next in your relationship, and that you both work towards a goal. It can be daunting to plan your future around another person, but it can do wonders for you both if we both work it through. Be vocal about your feelings so that the other person doesn't live in darkness about what you want.

Set An End Date
While long-distance love can be magical, but it's only a great thing for a finite time. Eventually, you would crave wanting to be in the same place as your partner. It can be hard to stay apart for a long time. One thing that'll help couples in this drastic time is to schedule a meeting and look forward to it every day. Both must stay equally committed to the

relationship and should be on the same page about how long this situation would last. You and your partner's plans should align in eventually living in the same place.

Do Stuff Together, Even Though You're Apart

If you aren't physically in the same place, it doesn't mean you both can't have fun together. You can plan a movie night via skype or cook something together while facetime-ing each other. There are loads of streaming services available that make it easier to binge-watch your favorite shows with your partner. Apart from that, you can also search for some quizzes or games online that will connect both of you and help you find more about each other. You can also raise controversial topics and spark new and exciting conversations to see your partner's stance.

Make Fun Plans For When You Both Will Meet

Indulge into details of what the two of you will do the next time you see each other. Make it a ritual of discussing all of the stuff with your partner that you so eagerly look forward to doing with them. Be it trying new restaurants every day, or picking up a holiday destination, or simply choosing a new hobby to do together. You can also schedule good night video calls in your PJs to create a sense of you going to bed together.

Set Clear Rules and Boundaries

Don'tDon't do anything that you wouldn't expect your partner to do either. Try your best to stay out of situations that might make your partner feel insecure or uncomfortable. You don't have to check in with your partner for every approval, but you should set clear boundaries for the both of you and adhere to them.

Conclusion

It can get lonely and difficult sometimes when dealing with long-distance but know that the fruits, in the end, will be as sweet as heaven. Constantly inject positive energy into your relationship to keep it alive. Be grateful for your partner and be thankful for the fact that there's someone who loves you and whom you love.

Chapter 4:
6 Signs Your Love Is One-Sided

While some things are better one-sided, like your favorite ice-cream cone that you don't want to share, your high school diary that knows all your enemies and crushes, and a game of solitaire. But a healthy relationship? Now that should be a two-sided situation. Unfortunately, when you're stuck in a one-sided relationship, it becomes easy to fool yourself every day that what you are experiencing is normal, when in reality, it could actually be toxic or even unworthy and loveless.

They could physically be sitting next to you, but you will find yourself being alone because of your emotional needs not being taken care of. Even though you have committed yourself to your partner, there's a fundamental difference between being selfless in love and giving it all without receiving anything at all. It might be possible that you're in denial, but the below signs of your one-sided love are hard to ignore.

1. **You're Constantly Second-Guessing Yourself**

If you don't get enough reassurance from your partner and constantly wonder if you are pretty enough, or intelligent enough, or funny enough, and always trying to live up to your partner's expectations, then you're definitely in a one-sided relationship. You tend to focus all of your energy and attention on being liked instead of being your true self and nurtured by your partner. It would be best if you always were your authentic self so the people who genuinely deserve you can get attracted to you and get relationships that match the true you.

2. You Apologize More Than Needed

Everyone makes mistakes. We are not some divine creatures who are all perfect and have no flaws. Sometimes you're at fault, sometimes your partner is. But if you end up saying sorry every single time, even if you had no idea about the fight, then maybe take a deeper look at your relationship. You may think that you're saving your relationship by doing this, but trust me, this is a very unhealthy sign. Cori Dixon-Fyle, founder and psychotherapist at Thriving Path, says, "Avoiding conflict results in dismissing your feelings." Solving fights should always be a team approach and not just one person's responsibility.

3. You're Always Making Excuses For Your Partner

Playing defense is excellent, but only on a soccer team. Suppose you are doing it constantly for your partner and justifying their behaviors to your circle of friends, family, and work colleagues. In that case, you're overlooking something that they are most likely seeing. If the people in your life are constantly alarming you, then maybe you should focus on your partner and see where the signs are coming from.

4. You Feel Insecure About Your Relationship

If you are never indeed at ease with your partner and often question the status of your relationship, then it's a clear sign that you are in a one-sided relationship. If you focus more on analyzing yourself, becoming more alluring, and choosing words or outfits that will keep your partner desiring you, then it's a major red flag. To feel unsettled and all-consumed in a relationship is not only exhausting, but it's also sustainable. Feeling constantly depleted in your relationship is also a sign that it's one-sided.

5. You're Giving Too Much

Giving too much and expecting just a little can never work in the long run. Suppose you're the only one in the relationship who makes all the plans. Do all the chores, remember all the important dates and events, consider stopping or making your partner realize that they aren't giving much in the relationship. Often when people give, they have some expectations in the back of their mind that the giving will be returned, but things fall apart when the other person never had those intentions. It's normal for a short while for one partner to carry the load more than the other; all relationships go through such stages, but constantly engaging in it is unhealthy.

6. You're Never Sure About How They Are Feeling

You can't read people's minds, nor are the communications transparent; you may end up overthinking their behaviors towards you and may be confused about how they're truly feeling. This uncertainty would cause you to dismiss your feelings in favor of thinking about them. This connection may be filled with guessing and speculations rather than knowing reality and seeing where they genuinely stand.

Conclusion

The best way to fix a one-sided relationship is to step away and focus on your self-worth and self-growth instead of trying to water a dead plant. You must focus on flourishing your own life instead of shifting your all to your partner. Your mental health should be your priority.

Chapter 5:
7 Ways To Become A Good Partner

Intro:

All relationships are unique. Different Experiences, personalities, interests, beliefs and culture tell us about the possibility of hundreds of different types of couples. However, some foundational qualities assure us of a lasting and healthy relationship no matter what kind of two people are involved. Whether you are in a relationship right now or you are single, you know what works for you, and you might be neglecting without even giving it a second thought. So, right now, what you should do is sit back, relax and think about what worked for you and what did not in your past relationships and what was lacking. You can also ask the people around you who are in committed relationships and what worked for them. Although the relationship dynamics of everyone are different, there is always something to learn. We are going to tell you a secret here. For a healthy and long-lasting relationship, you need to work on yourself first. We are going to list down 7 ways in which you can become a good partner.

1. **Be Secure Within Yourself:**

So often in your twenties, you feel like you are ready for a lasting relationship, but around that time, most people have not figured out what their passions are, or they are not confident enough. If you still have not figured out your outlet through which you will contribute to the world, and you are trying to lay the foundation of a new relationship, new home, chances are your relationship will not last long because you will feel restless all the time. However, once you have figured out your sense of being, it brings you a sense of contentment. It will be easier for you to maintain the balance between your work and your relationship. If you are secure with who you are, people's comments or words will not be able to bring you down. That can be difficult for people for various reasons, but you will have a happy relationship once you can do it.

2. **Be Responsible:**

You are going to have good days and bad days. There are going to be days where you will wake up sad and grumpy. After the emotion subsides, you should ask yourself what could be the reason for this. You should always take the responsibility of seeing the truth behind your emotion. Was it your partner's behaviour that made you feel left out or like a third wheel? Tell them. If you feel like your partner is taking advantage of your efforts and are working for this relationship as much as you do, talk to them about this. When you are in a relationship like this, these conversations are not always easy, but you need them to create a stronger bond.

3. Be Appreciative:

If you show appreciation for little things, it will strengthen your relationship. It could be as simple as calling them and letting them know when will you be home, making dinner or putting the garbage on the curb. All these little things show that you appreciate their existence in your life and are considerate of their time and feelings.

4. Laugh Together:

When you laugh as a couple, you open yourself up to your partner; this allows you to be vulnerable. When you can laugh at yourself and themselves in each other's presence, it will build trust towards each other that they will not judge, humiliate or capitalize but rather enjoy these small moments with you.

5. Spend Quality Time Together:

If you treat the relationship in your life as a priority, you will want to spend time together. Of course, there will be times when you will be socializing with others, but that will not give you moments of intimacy or bonding. Instead, you need to take time out to be together. You can have dinner at your favourite restaurant, watch a movie, cook dinner together, go hiking or just simply stay at home and watch Netflix and chill.

6. **Be Their Number One Fan:**

All of us can achieve amazing things in life, but when our loved ones appreciate us, it gives us a confidence boost when the people we love are standing behind us, supporting us as we work towards our goals. So as a partner, you need to understand your partner's dreams and goals and support them as they strive to achieve their goals, in good times and bad. You should let them know that you are always going to stand with them. When you know you have your partner's support, it is the best feeling in the world. But always remember, it is a two-way street.

7. **Be a Good Listen and Observer:**

Suppose you want to be a good partner. In that case, you must understand what annoys them. To do that, you should pay close attention to what they are saying. You need to listen to them and understand what makes them happy, what upsets them, but simultaneously you should be observing how they react in certain situations. What makes them nervous, and what makes them comfortable. You will get to know more about them by observing.

Conclusion:

We listed how you can be a better partner and make your special feel loved, but you should always remember that a relationship is a two-way street, and they should be putting in the same amount of effort. Make sure that your partner has not become lazy in love, and if you think one of you is getting there, you should have some activities that can bring things back on track, but you and your partner should have a mutual understanding.

Chapter 6:
6 Crazy Ways People Have Met Their Soulmates

DATING IS AN EXTREME SPORT, AND IT GETS MORE CHALLENGING WHEN WE HEAR ABOUT THE TRIALS AND TRIBULATIONS OF NOT FINDING "THE RIGHT ONE." DESPITE HOW COMPLEX THE DATING WORLD MAY BE, WE MAY SEE A GOOD PARTNER IF WE'RE LUCKY ENOUGH. WHEN IT COMES TO LOVE, PEOPLE TEND TO BELIEVE IN ALL SORTS OF THINGS, BE IT FATE, SOULMATES, LUCK, OR EVEN CLAIM THAT ONE LOOKS AT A PARTICULAR PERSON AND THEY WERE ASSURED THAT THEY WOULD SPEND THE REST OF THEIR LIVES WITH THEM. WHETHER YOU BELIEVE IN LOVE AT FIRST SIGHT OR ENJOY READING HOW COUPLES MET, HERE IS A LIST OF SOME CRAZY WAYS PEOPLE HAVE MET THEIR SOULMATES.

1. **Love on the high seas:**

A LONELY SWEDISH SAILOR NAMED AKE VIKING WROTE A LETTER TITLED "TO SOMEONE BEAUTIFUL AND FAR AWAY" ONE NIGHT. ONCE HE WAS DONE, HE PUT IT IN A BOTTLE AND TOSSED IT IN THE SEA, AND HOPED THAT FATE WOULD HELP HIM FIND THE LOVE OF HIS LIFE. AS COMMON SENSE WOULD DICTATE, THE BOTTLE SHOULD'VE BEEN DESTROYED OR WASHED UP ADRIFT ON SOME LONELY PIECE OF LAND. BUT, TWO YEARS LATER, AKE RECEIVED A REPLY FROM A YOUNG SICILIAN GIRL NAMED PAOLINA. THE TWO BEGIN WRITING LETTERS TO EACH OTHER, AND AKE DECIDES TO MOVE TO SICILY TO BE WITH PAOLINA.

2. Love at first flight:

MARSHA BOBB HAD A DATE WITH AMERICAN AIRLINES AND WALKED DOWN HER FLIGHT FROM JAMAICA TO MIAMI IN 2005. SHE SAW LENNY SPACE SITTING AT HER SPOT ON THE WINDOW SEAT AND DIDN'T LIKE IT ONE BIT. SHE WAS FORCED TO SIT IN THE OPEN CENTER SEAT. AT FIRST, SHE WAS GRUMPY WITH THE SITUATION, BUT SHE REALIZED HE WAS A DECENT FELLOW WHEN SHE TALKED TO LENNY. ON THE OTHER HAND, ONE LOOK AT MARSHA AND LENNY FELL HEAD OVER HEELS IN LOVE

WITH HER. THEY WOULD CHAT FOR HOURS TO NO END. THEY LOST TOUCH WITH ONE ANOTHER IN THE MIDDLE BUT GOT BACK AND NOW ARE MARRIED.

3. Facebook plays cupid:

WHEN FACEBOOK HAD ALL THE HYPE, A MAN NAMED SCHUYLER BENSON OF ARKANSAS TRIED TO LOG INTO THE WEBSITE ON HIS FLIP PHONE. THE PHONE GLITCHED, AND HE ACCIDENTALLY ACCESSED THE ACCOUNT OF A WOMAN NAMED CELESTE ZENDLER, WHO LIVED IN COLORADO. POOR SCHUYLER HAD NO IDEA WHAT TO DO AS FACEBOOK WOULDN'T LET HIM LOG OUT OF THE STRANGER'S ACCOUNT. THANKFULLY, HE WAS ABLE TO LOG OUT, AND HE SENT CELESTE A FRIEND REQUEST. AFTER THE GLITCH, THEY BOTH STARTED TALKING, MET IN PERSON, AND FELL IN LOVE. THE COUPLE GOT ENGAGED AND THEN GOT MARRIED.

4. A text leads to romance:

KASEY BERGH, A DIVORCEE FOR SIX YEARS, ACCIDENTALLY SENT A TEXT MESSAGE TO A STRANGER

WHILE SHE WAS IN DENVER WORKING ON A PROJECT FOR NESTLE-PURINA AND WAS ATTEMPTING TO CONNECT WITH OTHER EMPLOYEES. THE TEXT WAS SENT TO HENRY GLENDENING, WHO WAS STUCK IN AN UNHAPPY RELATIONSHIP AND A DEAD-END JOB. HE DIDN'T IGNORE THE TEXT MESSAGE BUT LET KASEY VENT ABOUT HOW FRUSTRATED SHE WAS TO BE STUCK IN DENVER AND UNABLE TO WORK ON HER PROJECT. THEY HIT IT OFF INSTANTLY AND EVENTUALLY FELL IN LOVE AND STARTED A RELATIONSHIP.

5. A match made in hospital:

DANNY ROBINSON AND HIS MOTHER APPEARED ON A RADIO SHOW TO SHARE HIS STORY ABOUT BEING DIAGNOSED WITH INFLAMMATORY KIDNEY DISEASE. AND IT JUST HAPPENED THAT ASHLEY MCINTYRE, WHO WAS DANNY'S AGE, OVERHEARD HER MOTHER AND GRANDMOTHER TALKING ABOUT THE YOUNG MAN'S TALE. ASHLEY AND DANNY SHARED THE SAME BLOOD TYPE, AND SHE DECIDED TO DONATE HER KIDNEY TO HIM AS SHE FELT COMPASSION FOR HIM. ASHLEY TURNED OUT TO BE THE PERFECT DONOR, AND DANNY INSTANTLY FELL IN LOVE WITH HER. THE TWO FAMILIES

GOT VERY CLOSE, AND DANNY STARTED A RELATIONSHIP WITH ASHLEY.

6. Marching into romance:

COLLEGE CAN BE A GREAT WAY TO MEET THE LOVE OF YOUR LIFE. A LADY WAS IN HER COLLEGE MARCHING BAND, AND THE GUY WAS HER SECTION LEADER. ONE DAY AT A FOOTBALL GAME, EVERYTHING CLICKED, AND THEY STARTED TALKING MORE AND MORE. THEY CREATED A RELATIONSHIP AND CONFESSED THEIR LOVE A WHILE LATER. THEY INDEPENDENTLY DECIDED TO GET MARRIED, AND SEVEN MONTHS LATER, THEY DID IT.

Conclusion:
NO MATTER WHERE IN THE WORLD YOU ARE, IF FATE HAS DECIDED TO LET YOU MEET YOUR SOULMATE, YOU DO MEET YOUR SOULMATE!

Chapter 7:
Make Time for Your Partner

When I first got into my relationship, I thought my boyfriend and my 100-hour workweek would have to battle it out until the bitter end. Yet somehow, I've managed to maintain both. It turns out there are a lot of weird ways to make time for your partner when you're busy AF. You may have to get creative and resort to some weird measures, but I am living proof that there is no such thing as being too busy for your loved ones.

We all have to run errands. That time is gone from your workday anyway. So, why not use it to show your partner you care instead of just getting what you need? Picking up each other's shampoo and favorite cereal (or, perhaps more practically, take turns picking up groceries and toiletries for the both of you) is one way to connect without needing to make any more time in your schedule.

You spend the same amount of time cooking for two people as you do for one, but since you're feeding two, you *save* time by doing this. Think about it: Instead of cooking every night, you only have to do it every *other* night. Even if you both eat it in front of your computers, making food for each other is a loving gesture that'll make you appreciate each other.

If you live together, you'll probably be sleeping in the same bed anyway. But even if you don't, your dates can consist solely of sleeping if that's what it takes to make time for each other. Or, if you can't sleep through the night with someone else next to you, you can try just sharing nap time.

Even if you don't get around to working out that much, the time you can devote to exercise will help clear your mind, so it's worthwhile if you can make it out for a short run or yoga class. Plus, [working out together can boost your attraction](#) by releasing endorphins.

I can't always handle this, especially when I need to feel like nobody wants my attention to focus. But for less intensive tasks, it can be comforting to cuddle up to your significant other while you're working. You can even be each other's sounding boards if you need help coming up with ideas.

This one will not work for everyone. But if you have an office in a similar place, your walk or ride to work can be your bonding time, even if it's just part of the way. Even just a shared walk to the train station can pay off if you think ahead enough to coordinate your trips to and from work.

Chapter 8:
7 Ways To Be More Mature In A Relationship

=

Intro:

Even if we love someone with all our heart, the reality of this life will be a reminder for us that nothing is ever as simple as it seems. You can ask anyone who has ever been in a relationship, and they will tell you that love is just one of the component you need for a committed relationship. But the important thing they will you that is essential for a relationship is maturity. Maturity is a skill that is not acquired from instinct and is instead learned. So, you might be wondering how one can act maturely in a relationship? Well, listen on, and you will get your answers.

1. Learn the values of respect, trust, and sincerity:

These are the essential ingredients of a healthy and happy relationship, and you should learn them as soon as you can. First, you need to trust your partner that they have the strength to fight for what you have. Second, you should appreciate their sincerity and also express genuine affection and love towards each other. Lastly, you should respect them as human being and as a person.

2. Address the needs of the relationship first:

When you are in a committed relationship, you are not thinking and making decisions for yourself and the other person, so there is no room for selfishness. Being mature in a relationship means working on your goals and making the right decisions that are beneficial for yourself and your partner. Whatever plans you have, they should be focused on the needs and wants of both of you because the consequences will affect not only your future but also theirs.

3. Accept the reality that people are not perfect:

When you get through your partner's bad moods and terrible tantrums and accept the worst parts of them, there is a huge chance that you guys are going to end up together. You have to accept the fact that the person you are in love with is not perfect; everyone has their flaws, and that is the beauty and complexity of a human, and once you accept that and see the beauty in them despite their flaws, that means you really love them, and that is also the mature move. However, you should always be aware that if they stoop too low, you should help them grow.

4. Practice patience and choose forgiveness:

The person you love can make you the happiest and at the same time break your heart in a million pieces. Love makes us vulnerable, and hence we get hurt easily. But you have to realize that just like you, your partner is only a human, and they can also make mistakes without realizing it. There can be moments when you will feel you are being taken for granted or that you have been betrayed, but you should not let these moments get to you. You should have patience, and that patience will give you strength, and when you forgive them, it will give you hope that everything is part of the process.

5. Relationships can't be perfect:

As we just mentioned, there will be days when the love of your life will break your heart or make you feel bad. And there are also going to be times when your wrong choices will affect your relationship or hurt your significant other. So, in those times, you should not lose hope and realize that no relationship is perfect and everything you are going through is just part of the process, and all the challenges you face will either make you or break you. But, you should be mature enough to not let them break you.

6. Recognize the power of words:

Words are extremely powerful; once you have said something, you can not take it back. Your words can make someone's day and can also make someone feel horrible about themselves. Therefore, you should make an active effort to learn what you should not express and what to say. Of course, you have the right to express whatever you are feeling, and it can be both good and bad, but you should never use this freedom to hurt the person you love the most.

7. Destructive consequences of overthinking:

One of the signs of maturity is to not let your destructive and damaging thoughts consume you. These destructive thoughts can ruin your relationship and even end it. Many younger couples do not have faith in their partners, which is the reason for their breakups, so it is important for mature adults to not act in the same way and let go of small things because, in the bigger picture, they will not matter.

Conclusion:

Life is difficult, and it takes a lot of time and maturity to figure it out and being in a relationship can make things complicated. So, even if you have lost someone because you were still figuring out things, you do not have to lose heart because you will soon find someone better.

Chapter 9:
7 Ways To Deal With An Overly Jealous Partner

Being jealous in a relationship seems cute at first, but it can really kill the love you and your partner have for each other after a while. You'll probably start to see the negative aspects of over jealousy pretty clearly. Some people have bad experiences and trust issues due to their past relationships, so being in a relationship with a jealous person shouldn't necessarily be a deal-breaker. It can be started by finding why your partner is feeling the way they feel, especially when you haven't given them a reason to mistrust you in the first place.

If your partner is being aggressive and trying to control what you're doing, you might want to try to work together with them to fix the issue. It will give them the reassurance they need and create a closer bond between you two. If your partner is turning red with jealousy lately, here are some signs for you to deal with them.

1. **Talk About Their Fears and Anxieties**

It would be best to calmly sit your partner down with you and ask them what's going on in their mind if you feel like your partner's jealousy is getting off the hook. Make sure you're listening to them fully attentively, and don't be scared to express how their thoughts affect you. Danielle B. Grossman, a California licensed marriage and family therapist, says, "Do not try to minimize, negate or 'fix' the fears. Do not try to bully your partner's fear into submission. Do not belittle, humiliate, shame, and threaten the fear." Always be empathetic and give them your undivided attention. Make sure you never attack your partner and make them trust that they can confide in you.

2. **Don't Get Defensive About Your Behavior**

If your partner is accusing you of something that is far from true, do not feed the fire by jumping right away into an argument. Evaluate the situation first. If you instantly try to get defensive, your partner will misinterpret your reaction or may get even angrier. Try to be patient first and deal with the situation calmly. Reassure them that whatever they're thinking isn't right, and you're always going to be with them no matter what.

3. **Be Extra Affectionate**

After discussing the reasons for their jealousy, show your partner extra love, during this weak and vulnerable time. This is the time to be more generous with your affection. Try to touch them more, make small gestures for them, and be supportive throughout this time. Of course, this means that you should take the abuse if extremely unhealthy jealousy is present. Don't let them force you into situations that you are uncomfortable dealing with.

4. Create Boundaries

Setting boundaries in your relationship isn't a negative thing at all. Loads of people in healthy relationships create a line to understand each other's emotions and priorities better. People should be aware of their selves even within a relationship. According to a Ph.D. psychologist Leslie Becker-Phelps, "You need to know what you like and dislike, what you're comfortable with versus what scares you, and how you want to be treated in the given situations." So, try your best not to let your mental health affect by your partner's conflicts.

5. Be Available and Responsive:

Although this issue is something that your partner needs to fix on their own, it can still help the situation get better if you're responsive when they reach out to you. If you're there when your partner needs you the most, and you tend to comfort them, it can help calm their jealous habits. This takes a lot of effort, without a doubt, but if your partner notices that you're available and receptive, then the trust between you two will only grow stronger with time.

6. Revisit The Issue and Be Patient

Over jealousy is an issue that can't be fixed overnight. You must be patient with your partner and show them now and then that you're willing to work on this problem together by supporting and discussing their fears. It can indeed be time-consuming and emotionally draining, but don't let it stop you from trying to work things out with your partner. Take baby steps, celebrate small victories until it isn't an issue anymore.

7. Rebuild Your Trust

If your partner is losing trust in you, make sure you gain it back by doing small things, such as facetiming them and texting them throughout the day, explaining to them why you're running late, or taking a rain check in advance if you know you're busy that day. Reassure them with positive statements, and this will eventually put your partner's fears at ease.

Conclusion

There's no magic spell or easy way to deal with a jealous partner, but if you want to make the relationship work, then put effort into it. Get your partner to trust you, be empathetic with them and talk about their feelings. This little bump in the road can probably go away, which will help you in the long run.

Chapter 10:
8 Signs That Someone Is Not Your Soulmate

When you find yourself in a relationship, everything feels fantastic. There are confused feelings everywhere, but those confusing feelings are just for the beginning. But we all do wonder if we'll ever find " the one." When we first enter a relationship, you may wonder if this is your soulmate. But sometimes, we want that one person to be our soulmate, but things just aren't meant to be that way. Here are a few signs that someone is not your soulmate.

1. **It is tough to trust them:**

If you feel yourself constantly spying about the whereabouts and motives of your partner because you feel like your partner is not honest with you, then you know that this person is not your soulmate. The reason behind this is that you can't just spend your whole life on the lookout. When you can't trust your soulmate no matter how much you try, you know that your partner is doing some shady stuff. A soulmate will be honest with their relationship even when you are not around because we all know, " Without trust, there is no relationship."

2. **You don't connect at an emotional level:**

In a relationship, you need to know all about your partner, about his life, his work, his future ambitions because if your connection with your partner is just surface level and you don't know anything about them, then you know that is not the "one." A soulmate would want to dig deeper into your soul and would want to know everything about you. Still, if you feel like they are not investing in the relationship and are not working for it, you may think that they are not interested in you or your life like a soulmate should be.

3. Your partner has different values than you:

Everyone has different values and meanings of life, but are these values too much further in your relationship? If so, then you know, this is not your soulmate. Indeed, a relationship requires compromise, but nobody can sacrifice too much, and having different values may as well result in that. Soulmates would have an essential, shared vision for the future.

4. He doesn't enhance your life:

A soulmate is someone who shows you a better side of yourself and life. A soulmate will make you feel complete, make you feel happy when you feel low, and give you the confidence you need. But if your partner makes no effort to help your personal growth or at least make you feel happy in your hard times, then you know that that is not your soulmate.

5. You wish to explore other interests:

It is entirely normal for a person that is in a relationship to find someone else attractive; after all, we all are human beings, but if you start picturing yourself with someone else and start wishing that you were single so you could explore other interests, then that is a huge sign you need to consider. When you find your soulmate, you would not wish to be single, and although other people still seem attractive, you would not want to leave your partner for them.

6. Your partner judges you:

All human beings have different views on life. Everybody thinks differently; indeed, there are things you and your partner do not have legal opinions on, and that is completely fine unless your partner starts judging you for doing something they don't like. Yes, a relationship does need compromise, but that surely does not mean that your partner gets the right to judge you because you did not compromise and still did something they don't like. A soulmate would never consider you for anything you do; a soulmate will understand you in the best possible way.

7. You don't feel the urge to text back:

Everybody knows that when you like someone, you reply to their messages as soon as you can. It is like a human being not to seem rude to the people they like, but if you don't want to reply to your partner, are you sure they are "the one"? If every other text you receive bothers you, and you don't feel that interested in them, you know that this person is not the one you were looking for.

8. **You don't just feel like telling him something important you:**

When you find the one, you want to tell them everything about yourself, including the essential things. But do you feel that way about your partner like you want to say everything about every day, or you just don't bother to tell? If you don't, then you know that he is not the one.

Conclusion:

Don't feel disheartened if you haven't found the right one yet because someone is made especially for you, and one day you will find your soulmate.

PART 3

Chapter 1:
6 Ways To Deal With Betrayal

Betrayal is a strong word. And the most challenging part of it is recovery. Healing from something someone has done to you that you were not in favor of can be as hard as counting the number of hair on your head. The first thing that comes in our way is our emotions. Anger, rage, and regret. But, what can one do to save themselves from such a move? They can only be careful with the people around them. Trust issues have always been challenging to deal with. And betrayal only fuels that fire. We often turn to others for support, and sometimes they turn out to be deceivers. It may leave us unprotected.

No doubt that betrayal changes someone to some extinct. The person may feel insecurities within themselves. They start to doubt and stress themselves. It often leads to self-harm, too, at times. And the most severe of them all would be anxiety. Because no matter what, we can't ignore the fact that someone has lied to us and made us believe them. Betrayal is painful. And it's common to have experienced it once in your life. When someone you trusted with your secrets or emotions has broken that trust, that feeling of not being valued enough makes us hate that person, whether they did it intentionally or unintentionally. But there can be some ways to deal with betrayal.

1. Take Time For Emotional Improvement

After a heartbreak, what we need is time. Time to think, time to process, and time to heal. We can't instantly forget about anything that has happened to us. "Time heals all wounds." And that is precisely what we should do. Take a break. Try to do things you want. Make yourself feel light and collected. Stay away from the person who hurt you. This way, it will help you bury that memory quickly. Try to think about it as little as possible. Make sure you have other things on your mind instead. Rearrange your priorities from the start. This time you believe in yourself more than you felt in that person.

2. Overcome Self-Hatred

It is often that you would feel hatred towards yourself. Because you sometimes believe that it was your fault, to begin with. The thing with betrayal is that it is one-sided. The other person can do nothing but suffer. Naturally, you would be pitying yourself for their actions and feeling insecure. But it's not worth your time or emotion. You need to get a hold of yourself and talk some sense into yourself.

3. Try To Forgive and Forget

We all know that it is not as easy as it sounds, but it is more beneficial. When someone betrays us, we feel the need to take revenge. Hurt them the way they hurt us. But nothing can be as comforting as forgetting it ever happened. We all will remember a part of it, but it doesn't have to come between your life. It takes a lot of determination to forgive someone you don't want to ignore, but you will see the pros of it in the future. If you decide you take revenge, then it will leave you guilty and regretful in the future.

4. Ask For Help From The Trusted

It may be difficult for you to trust anyone after being betrayed. But you can always go to someone for comfort. If a possible third party can support you, don't hesitate to reach out to them. Make sure you talk about it with someone so you can take advice and feel light. It will help you to deal with the situation quickly. It will give you the peace of mind that will help you all along the journey ahead. It is recommended to talk with someone who had a betrayal in their life.

5. Acknowledge, Don't React

There is a significant difference between responding and reacting. We should be in control of our emotions. We need to acknowledge our feelings. After betrayal, our senses are more likely to be mixed up, leaving us confused. But that is a recipe for disaster. It will only be harmful to you to react without analyzing the situation appropriately. You can't ignore the fact that you have been hurt, but you will feel calmer by the time.

6. Be Careful Next Time

No one can ensure that we won't get hurt again. But we can be careful around people. That doesn't necessarily mean having trust issues with people but detecting the people who can hurt you. And with each time, you will get better and better at dealing with betrayal. It would help if you felt those emotions to overcome them every single time. And after each series of betrayals, you will become stronger than before.

Conclusion

Betrayal can be heart-wrenching, but it should not stop you from being happy in life. Cry and grieve for a day or two. And then get up again as a stronger person. Believe in yourself. Let go of the past and focus on your future, for it can bring much more happiness.

Chapter 2:
7 Ways To Deal With Growing Apart In A Relationship

According to Ashley Davis Bush, LCSW, a psychotherapist who specializes in couple therapy, "It's incredibly easy for couples to grow apart because we have such busy lives." Change is inevitable. And while growing together is the vital key to last any relationship, we simply can't deny the fact that people evolve and change as time goes by.

If you go to sleep at night and wake up every morning knowing there's this one person in your life who loves you and has your back no matter what, then consider yourself very fortunate. But if you are in a relationship that has lost its passion or is struggling, you're probably suffering from the pain and frustration that's coming from the lack of love and support in your life. There could be a million reasons why your relationship isn't what it used to be. But the most common answer for the 80% of couples who get separated or divorced is, "we grew apart."

Here are 7 ways to deal with growing apart in a relationship.

1. Talk About It

Communication is the key to any healthy relationship. Let your partner know how you are feeling, and then get some ideas on how you both can get closer again. Being honest with your partner might work out brilliantly. You could start off by saying, "I really want to feel close to you again," or "it seems like we may be growing apart; how can we fix it?"

This will invite collaboration instead of the usual blame game. Maybe you will start to schedule more time together, get away for the weekend, or seek a couple of counseling. It's better to start off early than to wait till your whole relationship is damaged.

2. Bring Back Old Habits or Try Some New Ones

Sometimes you have to go down memory lane and recall the activities or things that brought both of you closer. Go into the flashbacks and see what helped you grow together? Maybe you both loved exercising together, or perhaps you both liked trying new restaurants. On the contrary, relationships thrive on novelty. You have to make sure that you're keeping things exciting and enjoyable by trying out new stuff.

3. **Ask Meaningful Questions**

Couples must remain interested in one another if they want to avoid growing apart. One of the many ways to do it is to deepen the conversation and allow access to the partner's inner thoughts and feelings. For example, if your partner is complaining about work, instead of suggesting solutions, ask them what would help them get through it and what they are feeling at that moment. You could ask about your partner's fears and doubts and appreciate them for everything they do for you.

4. **Be Curious About Your Partner's Needs and Behaviors**

It isn't easy to stay connected when one partner is a cat, and the other is a puppy. Meaning, one partner might need some space during the different needs closeness and reassurance. Over time, these slight differences could create conflict, frustration, and distance. But instead of giving into frustrations, trying being curious about what your partner wants. Try to get to the bottom of why your partner acts like that. Don't take their behaviors personally but instead assume the best and work towards making your partner and yourself feel relaxed and stress-free.

5. **Fight Productively**

Having good communication in your relationship also includes fighting productively. Couples shouldn't avoid conflict just because they don't want to get out of the honeymoon phase. By doing this, they suppress their feelings and emotions for fear of being different. Conflict is OK, but crossing the line while fighting or arguing isn't. Fighting the right way can help strengthen your bond, and it can also help you understand each other a lot more.

6. Be Kind To Each Other

One of the significant reasons to keep your relationship from growing apart is to be kind to each other. It's a simple thing, but many couples tend to overlook its importance with time. Being kind is as easy as complimenting your partner or doing something thoughtful for them. It's crucial to show kindness as much as you can. It can go a long way and helps make couples deposits in their love bank so that they can withdraw it and have fuel when the times are rough.

7. Practice Radical Acceptance

Practice the art of radical acceptance for having a long and happy partnership. This means that you should accept your partner as they are and resist the urge to fight the things that you can't change. Both partners should accept each other's imperfections, flaws, and quirks. Please stop trying to change their essential nature.

Conclusion

Maintaining a long-term relationship isn't easy. Many couples grow apart with time. But you have to understand that your relationship is like a gift in your life. You have to nurture it, be grateful for it, and do everything in your power to keep it thriving. If you're feeling distant in a relationship, the chances are that your partner is feeling the same. Be open with each other, and decide how you want to grow together.

Chapter 3:
What To Do When You Have Thoughts of Breaking Up

It's not always easy deciding if you should break up with your partner: You probably care about them and have many great memories together. But there could be real issues in the relationship that make you wonder if it's best to end things. Whatever outcome you settle on, however, it's a good idea to first ask yourself a few questions so you can be sure it's the right decision for you.

"Breaking up with your partner is the best thing to do if you feel like you're not happy anymore, and the relationship is just pulling you down instead of pushing you up.
Here are some things to think about before ending your relationship, according to experts.

1. Is There Anyone Influencing My Decision?

If you're seriously considering breaking up with your partner, it's wise to take a moment to think about what — or, more specifically, who —

might be influencing you toward this decision. Is your mom insisting you'd be better off without them? Does your best friend swear that splitting up is your best option? Although people's opinions can be a good guiding force, at the end of the day, this is your choice, not theirs.

2. Do We Hold the Same Core Values?

When you and your partner first got together, you might have initially bonded because you have similar interests. But if you're now at a place where you're thinking of taking the next steps or breaking up, it's worth asking yourself if the two of you align on values, too. "Preferences in daily life will change, but core values will likely not change. "You could feel like it is time to break up with your partner because those [incompatible] core values are showing themselves."

3. Would I Want My Child to Be With Someone Like My Partner?

It may seem like a strange thing to consider if starting a family isn't on the horizon, but it can be an effective litmus test to picture how you'd feel if your child were with someone like your partner. "This will trigger a reality check — would you want your children to spend the rest of their lives with the same kind of person as your partner? "If your answer is no, then take it as a sign that you are heading in the right direction ending the relationship."

4. Is This A Pattern for Me?

Are you someone who starts thinking of breaking up with your partner a few months in each time you're in a relationship? Do you start losing interest at about the one-year mark? Ask yourself whether this is a genuine impulse or if it's just a pattern for you. "Is the reason I desire to break up with someone unique to this person, or would it apply to multiple people?" Clara Artschwager, "If it applies to more than one person, this is often indicative of a larger limiting pattern in relationships."

Are you scared of getting too close to someone? Are you afraid of commitment? Reflecting on these things can help with your decision.

Chapter 4:
7 Ways To Deal With Sexual Problems In A Relationship

Whether the problem is big or small, there are as many things as you can do to get your sex life back on track. Your sexual well-being goes hand in hand with your overall emotional, physical, and mental health. Sexual dysfunction is defined as the difficulty or issue that might arise for an individual as well as for the couple during any stage of intimacy. It is an overly stigmatized situation that is far more common than many people realize. Overcoming sexual dysfunction doesn't have to be as daunting as it may feel. There are many ways to handle the frustration without putting too much strain on your partner or the relationship.

Communicating with your partner, availing yourself of some of the many excellent self-help materials on the market, maintaining a healthy lifestyle, and just having it easy and fun can help you weather tough times. Here are some ways to deal with the sexual problems in your relationship.

1. **Know The Importance of Intimacy**

It is essential to notice when the intimacy starts to wane within their relationship. Couples need to understand that they won't have the same level of sexual drive or desires throughout their relationship. Intimacy is a significant element to help couples bond. We feel calm and connected when we experience love and physical contact. If you have started to feel like you and your partner are experiencing intimacy issues, address them and don't hide them out of sheer embarrassment and shame.

2. **Remember That You Are Not Alone**

Sexual dysfunction in all its forms is something that plagues countless couples. There's no need to feel isolated. There are always ups and downs in every couple's sex life, and the real problem arises when they don't know how to talk about sex or the issues related to it. The societal stigma surrounding sexual dysfunction and lack of communication skills and education serve as the basis for why the couples feel ashamed and isolated in addressing their issues.

3. **Get Educated**

Couples mainly set up unrealistic expectations about sex that lead them to nothing but disappointment. Couples need to realize that their sexual desires, preferences, and abilities will begin to change as they age. A couple should get themselves informed about sexuality, sexual intercourse, and sexual dysfunction to be well aware of the challenges that they are facing or might face ahead. An excellent way to get educated is by contacting a sex therapist or reading books if you are too shy to talk openly about it.

4. Don't Play The Blame Game

Suppose the challenges you're facing affect one partner only. In that case, it is significant to face the issue as a team and work through it together. It is critical to look at sexual dysfunction as a couple experiencing a problem, and not just one partner. There is nothing worse than blaming and isolating your partner. Without the said support and communication, the problem is more likely to be increased than to dissolve.

5. Communicate With Care

Don't attempt to discuss your sexual problems with your partner if they are already stressed out about something else. Remember, timing is everything. Carefully address the problem with your partner and choose soft words to convey your message. Before engaging in the discussion, make sure both of you are level-headed, calm, well-rested, and prepared to have the conversation. It could get quite emotional, so you both have to be careful.

6. Give Yourself Time

As you age, your sexual responses slow down, and it may need more time for you to get aroused. The physical changes in your body might now give a completely different perspective of your sexual desires and arousals. Working on these physical necessities into your lovemaking routine can open doors to a new kind of sexual experience for you.

7. Do Kegel Exercises

Improving sexual fitness is essential for both men and women. They can do so by exercising their pelvic floor muscles. To engage in these exercises, tighten the muscle you would use to stop the urine in midstream. Hold the contraction for 2-3 seconds and then release. Repeat this ten times, doing a set of five each day. These exercises can be done anywhere, whether driving, standing in a checking line, or sitting at home.

Conclusion

Sexual dysfunction might be one of the hardest things to overcome in a relationship and is undoubtedly one of the most challenging issues to communicate with your partner about. However, with a bit of hard work, and a lot of support and love from your significant other, there is always a hope that you and your partner will find a solution that will eventually bring back happiness into your lives.

Chapter 5:
6 Signs You Have A Fear of Intimacy

Intimacy avoidance or avoidance anxiety, also sometimes referred to as the fear of intimacy, is characterized as the fear of sharing a close emotional or physical relationship with someone. People who experience it do not consciously want to avoid intimacy; they even long for closeness, but they frequently push others away and may even sabotage relationships for many reasons.

The fear of intimacy is separate from the fear of vulnerability, though both of them can be closely intertwined. A person who has a fear of intimacy may be comfortable becoming vulnerable and showing their true self to their trusted friends and relatives. This problem often begins when a person finds relationships becoming too close or intimate. Fear of intimacy can stem from several causes. Overcoming this fear and anxiety can take time, but you can work on it if you know the signs of why you have the fear in the first place.

1. **Fear Of Commitment**

A person who has a fear of intimacy can interact well with others initially. It's when the relationship and its value grow closer that everything starts to fall apart. Instead of connecting with your partner on an intimate level, you find ways and excuses to end the relationship and replace it with yet another superficial relationship. Some might even call you a 'serial dater,' as you tend to lose interest after a few dates and abruptly end the relationship. The pattern of emerging short-term relationships and having a 'commitment phobia' can signify that you fear intimacy.

2. Perfectionism

The idea of perfectionism often works to push others away rather than draw them near. The underlying fear of intimacy often lies in a person who thinks he does not deserve to be loved and supported. The constant need for someone to prove themselves to be perfect and lovable can cause people to drift apart from them. Absolute perfectionism lies in being imperfect. We should be able to accept the flaws of others and should expect them to do the same for us. There's no beauty in trying to be perfect when we know we cannot achieve it.

3. Difficulty Expressing Needs

A person who has a fear of intimacy may have significant difficulty in expressing needs and wishes. This may stem from feeling undeserving of another's support. You need to understand that people cannot simply 'mind read,' they cannot know your needs by just looking at you;

this might cause you to think that your needs go unfulfilled and your feelings of unworthiness are confirmed. This can lead to a vicious cycle of you not being vocal about your needs and lacking trust in your partner, and your relationship is meant to doom sooner or later.

4. Sabotaging Relationships

People who have a fear of intimacy may sabotage their relationship in many ways. You might get insecure, act suspicious, and accuse your partner of something that hasn't actually occurred. It can also take the form of nitpicking and being very critical of a partner. Your trust in your partner would lack day by day, and you would find yourself drifting apart from them.

5. Difficulties with Physical Contact

Fear of intimacy can lead to extremes when it comes to physical contact. It would swing between having a constant need for physical contact or avoiding it entirely. You might be inattentive to your partner's needs and solely concentrate on your own need for sexual release or gratification. People with a fear of intimacy may also recoil from sex altogether. Both ends of the spectrum lead to an inability to let go or communicate intimately emotionally. Letting yourself be emotionally naked and bringing up your fears and insecurities to your partner may help you overcome this problem.

6. You're Angry - A Lot

One way that the deep, subconscious fear of intimacy can manifest is via anger. Constant explosions of anger might indicate immaturity, and immature people are not able to form intimate relationships. Everyone gets angry sometimes, and it's an emotion that we cannot ignore, even if we want to. But if you find that your feelings of anger bubble up constantly or inappropriately, a fear of intimacy may be lurking underneath. Don't deny these intimacy issues, but instead put them on the table and communicate effectively with the person you are interested in.

Conclusion

Actions that root out in fear of intimacy only perpetuate the concern. With effort, especially a good therapist, many people have overcome this fear and developed the understanding and tools needed to create a long term intimate relationship.

Chapter 6:
7 Ways To Achieve Harmony In Personal Relationships

How beautiful the world or life would be if we were all blessed with harmonious relationships. The kind that is selfless, giving, and nurturing, the kind that doesn't have any tussle of egos and power play. Just you and your significant other fitted together, like a hand in the glove. Harmony isn't an inherent trait; that is one of the reasons why it becomes too difficult for relationships to flow seamlessly. Here are some tips and tricks to build a harmonious relationship with others.

1. **Harmony Can Be Nurtured**

Before getting into the ways to let go of all the negativities and build a holistic, harmonious relationship, we must first understand why harmonious relationships are essential. A harmonious person is defined as someone who is easygoing and has the ability to get along well with others. A harmonious bond is something that two people experience without fighting, clashes, or ego tussles. But most of the time, one of the partners might feel negative emotions, which can affect the quality of the relationship. Feeling discontent in a relationship might have distressing and overwhelming experiences, but that does not in any way means that we should lose all hope.

2. **Be the best version of yourself:**

If you look into your personal relationships to compensate for your loneliness, you are bound to get disappointed sooner or later. It indeed takes two to tango, but building a relationship and making sure it lasts has a lot to do with your state of mind. You have to be peaceful with yourself first before achieving peace in your personal relationships. Over-expecting things from your partners or others would always lead to disappointment, which will, in turn, channel into challenges and difficulties in your relationship. You have to be the bearer of harmony that you wish to cultivate in your relationships. You can start by fixing the broken things on your end, and others will eventually follow you.

3. **Embrace acceptance:**

Resistance and harmony can never go hand in hand. If you wish to achieve harmony, you have to let go of resisting the current order of things or change. Resistance can be in the form of criticizing your partner for whatever behaviors and traits they possess and forcing them to change who they are. This would lead to negativity and tension in the relationship. Going from resistance to acceptance is a passable road that will lead you towards building a harmonious relationship. You have to be aware that no one is perfect, even ourselves. We are bound to make mistakes and have flaws and have to accept others and their defects and errors.

4. Let go of the hurt and negativity:

Sometimes, it's our baggage of the past that keeps us unable to build a harmonious relationship. For example, it might be something that your ex-partner did to immensely hurt you, or a family member criticized you. However, you didn't process this hurt nor gave it the time to heal, but instead decided to bottle up your decisions and move on. It is only natural that the negative feelings you are keeping inside you for a long time will come out when someone bad triggers you. In this case, you have to find a way to let go of whatever hurt you're feeling, channel all your negativity, and foster harmony in your relationships.

5. Practice compassion:

You have to internalize gentleness and compassion, both as an individual and a couple if you want to build a close and harmonious relationship. When you address and approach any conflict and issue with gentleness, your mind will automatically respond with empathy rather than jumping to conclusions. This will facilitate open communication and inhibitions. It will also enable you to view the other person's perspective and views with kindness. This would put you in a position to give your partner space to process their thoughts and emotions.

6. Free yourself from expectations:

The stringent expectations we might feel from our loved ones can take a toll on our equation with them. While it is only natural to expect some things from the people we love, we shouldn't set them in stone. Because unmet expectations lead to a handful of negative emotions of disappointment, hurt, and anger, you end up saying hurtful things to other people. Instead of expecting too much, accept them as they are, allow them to be their own person, and appreciate the good they bring into the relationship. Appreciate their efforts even if they don't go your way.

7. Give and seek space in your relationships:

Personal space is one of the rarest yet one of the most crucial elements of feeling at peace in your relationships. Oftentimes, we get so much tethered with our loved ones that it feels like a permanent embrace. It may seem exciting and comforting at first, but soon it will leave you guys feeling suffocated from each other. We must understand that everyone needs their space t catch a breath, reflect, unwind and grow. It is also a hallmark of a healthy bond. To build a harmonious relationship, you must dismantle the clingy approach and give each other all the space you need.

Conclusion:

A harmonious relationship needs sustained efforts and nurturing, and you can neither expect to achieve harmony overnight nor do expect it to last forever once achieved. But it is sure is worth every effort. The importance of building a harmonious relationship lies in the fact that it brings you peace and hope, the two things most vital to any individual.

Chapter 7:
6 Ways To Be More Confident In Bed

Confidence is something a lot of people inherit naturally, while others could work on. When you're confident and comfortable in your skin, people assume that you have a reason to be, and then they react and respect you accordingly. You can be confident all you want at work or on dates, but what about being confident in bed? Being confident sexually can be enjoyable for both you and your partner. It isn't just at ease sexual, but also it's comfortable with the way you express and experience your sexuality.

Sexual confidence can be measured by how authentically you can relate intimately either with yourself or your partner and how pure and vulnerable you are in that sexual space where you feel like giving your 100 percent to be yourself and communicate the pleasure you desire. Building your confidence in bed can crucially improve your sex life. Here are some tips on how to be more confident in bed.

1. **Do What You're Already Confident In**

Even if you are insecure and think you lack sexual skills, there must be at least a tiny thing that you might be good at. Maybe you don't feel confident enough about your kissing skills, but you're a great cuddler, or perhaps you feel shaky about touching and teasing but are good vocally. Focus on what you're good at and polish that skill every time you're in bed with your partner. This will help you boost your confidence and might even convince you to try something new with them.

2. Try Something New

Once you start considering yourself as the master of that one skill you have been practicing, you would end up craving to try new things. Start with the things you're less comfortable with; maybe stepping out of your comfort zone might be enjoyable for you after all. You neither have to perfect the skill nor be a master of it, just trying it out can be fun in itself. It might be helpful to broaden the sexual script so that it doesn't look the same every time and bore your partner, but instead, trying new things can be an excellent adventure for you as well as your partner.

3. Laugh It Off If You Trip Up

You can't be good at everything you try in bed, nor should you be. What matters is how well you keep your attitude, and if you can have fun with it and have a great laugh if things go south, that's an achievement in itself. If you have already built up consistent self-confidence, then you can laugh it out loud on something that you can't get a grip on. After all, there might always be some things you'll be bad at and others in which you'll be a master.

4. Focus On What You Love About Your Body

There are instances where we will be utterly insecure about our bodies and features. There are some physical traits that we don't like but have made peace with, while others that we want but don't appreciate enough. The next time you look in the mirror, focus more on what you like about your face and body, be confident in them, and the things you don't like about yourself will vanish automatically.

5. Wear What Makes You Feel Confident

There is no particular stuff you have to wear or the way you have to look to feel more confident, but if you wear a look that you think looks great, you must go with it. Chances are, you will start feeling better about yourself instantly. If you feel more confident wearing lipstick, then wear it to bed, or if you think sexier wearing a lotion, use it before bed. Do whatever makes you feel like a total hottie.

6. Repeat A Mantra

We have all heard of the phrase "fake it till you make it." So, there's no harm in faking affirmations till you start believing in them. Keep repeating "I'm confident, I've got this" till it gets through. Affirmations increase how positively we feel about ourselves.

Conclusion

The task of becoming confident may seem daunting, but these small sub-tasks are an easy way to start. Another plus point is once you have practiced these techniques in bed, the confidence will spill over into every area of your life.

Chapter 8:
6 Steps To Recover From A Breakup

Breakups are tough to go through. Even when they end with good terms, it still brings out many insecurities and traumas of the past. These include the fear of abandonment, loneliness, etc. Breakups have become a prevalent thing for us, so familiar that we sometimes forget how painful it can be. When you have imagined your whole future with someone, and someone ends up leaving you, you feel broken, but you would know it happened for a reason. Recovering from a breakup is not an impossible thing to do, and most of us recover from a partition even if it may take some time. Here are a few steps to recover from a breakup.

1. **Talk About It**

After a breakup, everything seems to be falling apart, and it is tough to talk about it, about the pain it has caused. But it is scientifically proven that talking about your breakup helps you recover from it; as you start talking about it, you are reminded about what went wrong. This enables you to understand that it was for good. When you talk about it to others, they tell you their perspective, and you start to see things from a different point of view; this way, you understand what went wrong, and you begin to feel more okay with things.

2. **Keep A Journal**

Even though talking helps, sometimes we can't find the right person to talk to, who will understand us. In a situation like this, you can always start journaling; it is an emotional release, where you write about your feelings, where you pour your heart out. You will feel more comfortable because no one will judge you; as you start writing, your hands would automatically write something that would surprise you, but those surprising things will help you figure yourself out.

3. **Write Again and Again**

When journaling, act as if you are telling all these things to a stranger and don't stop just then, write again and again as if you are talking to a different stranger every time you write about your breakup, it will help you gain a different perspective, you would realize many things, but above all, you would learn that whatever happened, happened for a better tomorrow.

4. **Let It All Out**

When going through a breakup, we all want to scream, shout and let all the anger out, but of course, you can't do all these things in public. So take some time out for yourself, go somewhere private, and talk all the anger, frustration, and tears out. It is normal to feel this way after a breakup, but remember that bottling up your emotions is never good. On the other hand, letting it all out helps you a lot; this would reduce the pressure of all your feelings.

5. Stick To Your Routine

When going through a hard time, we stop following our daily routine, sure it is okay to take some time off from work, but it is not okay to stop eating. When going through a heartbreak, many people stop eating correctly, start sleeping more in the mornings, and just kind of mess their routine. But now is the time to work on yourself, don't stop eating healthy, don't mess up your sleeping habits, and above all, start going to the gym; you can let all the anger and frustration out through some exercise.

6. It Is Time To Make Yourself Feel Special

After a breakup, your sense of self-worth is reduced, a lot of insecurities attack you, but this is not the time to hate yourself; it is the time to love yourself. Don't just sit at home, watching a movie and crying about your breakup; what you can do is get a change. You can go shopping, buy new clothes, jewelry, etc. Get a new haircut, and love the new you. Focus on yourself, become selfish for a while. Now you don't have to think about anyone else, set new goals, and above all, take care of yourself.

Conclusion

Breakups have become very common, so familiar that people sometimes forget what it feels like, but don't worry, and you were not born with this person, try to work on yourself and give yourself the love you deserve. Remember that you are worth someone who cares about you and loves you the way you want to be loved. It is okay to be single; it is the time to try new things and redefine yourself.

Chapter 9:
6 Signs You Are Ready To Move To The Next Step In A Relationship

If you're dating someone long enough, chances are you might know them well now and are ready to take your relationship to the next level. You both work out well together through all the ups and downs, connect with each other, and make each other's life wonderful. So whether you're thinking about making your relationship official by introducing them to your family and friends, moving in with them, or even getting engaged, it can both be scary and exciting when you think about making the relationship serious and taking that leap of faith.

If you feel that you have a healthy relationship, you can't imagine your life without your partner and are in a good place emotionally, then say no more. Here are some signs to convince you that you should up your game!

1. **You Both Trust Each Other Fully**

Being able to trust someone entirely isn't as easy as it sounds, especially in times like these and the world we're living in right now. The most significant quality one can look for in a partner is how much they value our trust. If you are confident that your partner will always have your back and you can be weak and vulnerable in front of them, maybe you should consider taking the next step. If you have told something to them in confidence and they don't share the information with anyone, and likewise if you do the same, then you both are fortunate.

2. You Support Each Other Through The Good and Bad

Having someone by your side who you know would always support you, no matter what is nothing short of a blessing. Your partner has always comforted and consoled you through the negative phases and cherished and cheered you through the positive ones. Even if they were dealing with their problems, they made sure you were okay first. Most of the time, we tend to emotionally drain out or become frustrated by being there for people. But with your partner, you are always ready to lend a helping hand and even an ear, listen to all of their problems and shortcomings and support them every step of the way.

3. You Both Apologize To Each Other When Needed

One of the major signs of a toxic relationship is when your partner doesn't apologize or take accountability, even if they know they are wrong. These relationships tend to have a dead end. You might have noticed that your partner admits when wrong and apologizes, even if not straight away; they do it sooner or later. They try to sort out the arguments and fights calmly and try to listen to your point of views and opinions too, instead of forcing theirs on you. They make sure that you're okay after the fight and may even make small gestures to make you feel that they are guilty and you are more important than any of the arguments you both get into.

4. You Give Each Other Space

You both have a level of freedom and independence both within and outside the relationship. You both aren't on each other's throat and nerves every second. You both have different hobbies and passions that you pursue. You both can meet your friends alone or hang out by yourself, without stressing over if your partner would mind. This is a sign of a healthy relationship when you don't keep buzzing your partner with unlimited calls or texts, ask them about their whereabouts, or cling to them all day.

5. You're On The Same Page With Them

Even if you and your partner don't share the same goals, hobbies, dreams, passions, or even the same views and opinions, you're still on the same page with them about your values and future. For example, both of you have discussed either having children or no children in the future, getting a destination wedding or a simple one, moving out of the city or across the country, or settling in the same spot where you both are right now. Agreeing on the same stuff shows that you both prioritize the same things and are compatible with stepping up your relationship.

6. You Feel Safe With

One of the signs that your relationship is ready for the next step is the feeling of comfort and security when you are with them. You can be your utter authentic self with them without fearing that they might judge you or dislike you. You have shown all of your sides to them, the good and the bad, and they still love you regardless. They like your quirks and don't get annoyed or irritated by your behavior. You also have accepted your partner's flaws and imperfections and still look at them the same way.

Conclusion

Taking the next big step in a relationship could be confusing and stressful, especially when you find yourself confused and unclear. So if you have found someone worthy of your time and energy, don't let them go. Instead, cling onto them, and make efforts to keep your relationship floating.

Chapter 10:
7 Signs You Have Found A Keeper

Are you looking for Mr. or Mrs. Right? Or do you think you have found the right person, but how can you be sure? Sometimes, we meet someone who seems like the person you would want to spend your whole life with, but during those times, someone is in for a quick hookup. The only partners worth keeping are the ones that give you the positive vibes that you need after a dull and tedious day, the ones that make you feel happy, and your relationship doesn't feel boring at all. Here are signs that you have found a keeper.

1. **They inspire you to become a better person:**

When we meet someone very kind, helpful and overall a friendly person that person usually inspires us to be better and luckily the world is full of friendly people. Is your partner like this too? Is he warm, kind, and helpful? Does he inspire you to become a better version of yourself? Then you know you have found yourself a keeper. You know you have found the right person when your partner works hard, gives you and his family time, and has his life organized.

2. **They are always there:**

There are times when we all suffer when things get tough to handle. At times like these, a person always needs support and love to get through the hard times. If your partner is there for you even when you can't defend yourself and they cheer you up, you know that this is a keeper. A perfect partner is someone who knows how to make you laugh even when you are crying, your partner will never believe the things people talk about behind your back, and he would never hesitate to lend you a hand when you need some help.

3. **They know you more than yourself:**

Sometimes it fascinates us how someone can know us more than we know ourselves; it feels perfect when someone knows how or what we are thinking. If your partner knows what you are feeling without telling them, then they are the one. Does your partner know what you are comfortable with? Can they tell when you feel upset? Do they motivate you to do better and ask you to chase after your dreams? If so, then don't waste more time thinking if this is the right person for you because it is.

4. **Your interests are common:**

Sure, opposites attract, but too many differences are not usually suitable for someone's relationship. It would help if you had a common interest with your partner, like having common beliefs, values, and religious perspectives. When you agree on these things, your bond will become more robust, and you would find it very easy to live with that person.

5. **They are honest with you:**

Finding an honest person is a tiring thing to do; many people lie more than twice a day, but how can that affect your relationship? The right one may lie about small things that don't matter that much, like whether the color suits you or not; they may say those things to make you feel good about yourself, but lying about other things like financial status, health, or fidelity can be more serious. A true keeper would never keep these things from you, and they would always be honest with you even if the truth upsets you.

6. **They don't feel tired of you:**

Although everyone needs some space, even from the person they love the most, he will never get tired of you if he is the one. Your partner will never feel bored with you; on the contrary, your partner will never get tired of looking at you, admiring you, being with you, and above all, love you. When a person is so in love with you that they want to spend every second of their life with you, then you know you have found a keeper.

7. You are a part of their dreams:

Can your partner not even imagine your life without you? Has your partner already planned his future, and you are a big part of it? If so, you know that this one's a keeper. You both have reached a point in your lives where even thinking about living without each other sounds absurd, and then you know that you have found a keeper.

Conclusion:

A keeper is someone that loves, cherishes, and cares for you like no one has ever had. Don't worry if you haven't found your keeper, and it is just a matter of time before you do because, for every one of us, there is someone out there.

www.ingramcontent.com/pod-product-compliance
Lightning Source LLC
Chambersburg PA
CBHW071738080526
44588CB00013B/2073